# The Book of Numbers

D0931974

# The Book of Numbers

## An Exposition by
## Charles R. Erdman

**BAKER BOOK HOUSE**
Grand Rapids, Michigan 49506

ISBN: 0-8010-3378-0

PHOTOLITHOPRINTED BY CUSHING - MALLOY, INC.
ANN ARBOR, MICHIGAN, UNITED STATES OF AMERICA

*We are journeying unto the place of which the Lord said, I will give it you; come thou with us, and we will do thee good; for the Lord hath spoken good concerning Israel.*

NUMBERS 10:29

# *Introduction*

THE BOOK of Numbers is much more than a muster
roll of the armies of Israel. It does contain two such
numberings of the people, one recorded in the opening chapters and another in the twenty-seventh chapter; but the substance of the book is a record of the
events which occurred between this first and second
census. Indeed, Numbers is a history of the wilderness
experiences of the Children of Israel. Therefore, a
more exact title may be that which is found in the
Hebrew Bible, namely, "In the Wilderness," a phrase
which is taken from the first verse of the first chapter.
The time covered by the Book is nearly forty years, yet
it is surprising to note that the narrative is confined
to only the events that occurred in the second and
the fortieth years of this wilderness sojourn.

As the story opens, Israel is encamped at Mount
Sinai. Under the leadership of Moses the people have
been delivered from bondage in Egypt and at the
foot of the sacred mountain have entered into a covenant with Jehovah, promising to recognize him as
King and to be obedient to His laws. This deliverance from bondage and this covenant are recorded
in the Book of Exodus, which closes with an account
of the Tabernacle erected as a place for divine worship. In the Book of Leviticus which follows there is
given to the priests and Levites a handbook contain-

7

ing the prescribed ritual for worshipers. Yet the Israelites were to be not only worshipers but warriors. Therefore, in the first chapters of the Book of Numbers there is an account of the mustering and the organization of the people in preparation for the journey to Canaan and for the conquest of the land.

The next ten chapters deal chiefly with the march to the southern borders of Canaan and the repulse at Kadesh. The remaining chapters relate to the events of the fortieth year, including the conquest of territory east of the Jordan and the encampment on the plains of Moab in readiness to take possession of the Land of Promise.

Many readers of this rather neglected Book of Numbers will be surprised at the familiarity and fascination of its narratives. All remember something about the "pillar of cloud and of fire," the heroism and humility of Moses, the courage of Joshua and Caleb, the jealousy of Miriam and Aaron, the rebellion of Korah, the water from the riven rock, the serpent of brass, the strange story of Balaam, and the Cities of Refuge. The frequent repetition of these narratives has not detracted from their charm. They give a unique portrayal of the character and conduct of the nation. It is a story of the cowardice and heroism, the weakness and nobility, the defeats and victories, the sins and repentance of a historic people. The epic simplicity, the evident honesty and the high morality of these records have given them a permanent place in the literature of the world.

Yet the Book of Numbers is not merely a chapter of ancient history. It is a rich contribution to religion. It is a commentary on the nature and providences of God. The narratives are interspersed with laws, and both the records and the statutes reveal a King who delivers, who guides, who protects, and who sustains His people. He is a King of righteousness, of justice, of holiness and grace. When the people are disobedient and rebellious He punishes them; when they repent, He pardons and restores. His whole purpose in His dealings with them is to bring them into closer fellowship with Himself and to enrich their lives as His own "purchased possession." The Book of Numbers may be defined as a Drama of Divine Discipline.

However, the book is not only a record of past religious experiences; it is a guide for the people of God in the present day. It is rightly interpreted in the light of the New Testament revelation. Its highest service is found by regarding it as a book of types and symbols and object lessons designed for the instruction of the followers of Christ. In referring to these wilderness experiences of Israel, the Apostle Paul declares, "Now all these things happened unto them for ensamples: and they are written for our admonition, upon whom the ends of the world are come" (I Cor. 10:11).

With no undue flights of fancy, the hosts of the redeemed may find in these narratives warning and guidance and inspiration as they journey through the "wilderness of this world," guided by "the pillar of cloud," nourished by "the bread which came down from heaven," quenching their thirst with water from "the riven rock," encountering enemies, fighting battles and ever pressing onward toward the Land of Promise, the "inheritance of the saints in light."

# Contents

12 CONTENTS

*The Book of Numbers*

# I

## *PREPARATIONS FOR THE MARCH*

### NUMBERS 1:1 to 10:10

### THE NUMBERING AND ORGANIZATION OF THE PEOPLE [Chs. 1 to 4]

WHEN the hosts of Israel swept across the peninsula of Sinai to secure a home in Canaan they were not to be thought of as a mere mob of fugitive slaves. After months of anticipation they had been led forth from Egypt in "orderly array." During a year spent at the foot of the Holy Mountain they had been more fully organized for the wilderness journey and for the conquest of the Land.

The most important feature of this further preparation was *the numbering of the people.* This was undertaken by divine command, "on the first day of the second month, in the second year, after they were come out of the land of Egypt." As divinely instructed, Moses and Aaron, to assist them in their task, selected twelve chieftains, each one the representative of a tribe. They are described as "the renowned of the congregation, princes of the tribes of their fathers, heads of thousands in Israel." Under their direction the people "declared their pedigrees after their families, by the house of their fathers, according to the number of the names, from twenty years old and upward, by their polls." This was to say, each individual was enrolled under three heads, (1) according to his tribe, (2) according to his family, (3) according to his father's house.

However, this was not a complete census of the nation. It was the muster roll of the army. It included only "every male from twenty years old and upward, all that were able to go forth to war."

When one seeks in the history of Israel for types of Christian experience, it is well to be reminded that the followers of Christ are not only "wayfarers in a wilderness" journeying to a "better country," but also are "soldiers of the cross," called to fight "against principalities, against powers, against the rulers of this world's darkness, against spiritual wickedness in heavenly places." They are commanded to "put on the whole armor of God," and to "fight the good fight of faith," and to "lay hold on the life eternal."

Each of the twelve tribes in order was carefully enrolled and the sum total of its warriors recorded. It is of interest to note that the tribe of Judah was the largest in number, and to recall that hundreds of years earlier Jacob had predicted of Judah, "Thou art he whom thy brethren shall praise" (Gen. 49:8). So, too, Ephraim outnumbered Manasseh; and thus Jacob, in blessing his grandsons, had set Ephraim before Manasseh; to this Joseph, their father, had objected; and the reply had been made: "Manasseh also shall become a people, and he also shall be great, but truly his younger brother shall be greater than he" (Gen. 48:19, 20).

After the separate enumerations, the total number of the twelve tribes was announced: "six hundred and three thousand and five hundred and fifty." If it is calculated that each warrior represented three or four noncombatants, the entire host of Israelites may have numbered something like two million souls. To suppose that so many men and women, together with flocks and herds, could have survived in the wilderness of Sinai for a period of forty years, does involve serious difficulties. It is understood, however, that the people did not remain together continually in one place, but scattered widely over the peninsula, parts of which were fertile and cultivated. Nor is it known what changes in physical conditions the region has undergone during the passing of three thousand years. Most important of all, allowance must be made for miraculous supplies of food and water. Whatever attitude one may take toward the record of supernatural events, it is evident that acts of divine intervention form an integral part of the historic narrative.

One tribe was omitted in this muster roll of the army; this was the *tribe* of *Levi*. The members of this tribe were assigned to the tabernacle as ministers of religion. The divine command was as follows: "But appoint thou the Levites over the tabernacle of the testimony, and over all the furniture thereof, and over all that belongeth to it: they shall bear the tabernacle, and all the furniture thereof; and they shall minister unto it, and shall encamp round about the tabernacle."

The Levites "were not numbered among" the fighting forces, yet they were separately and even more fully enrolled, not "from twenty years old and upward," but "from a month old and upward" (Ch. 3:15). They held among the tribes a place of conspicuous honor. For their support all other Israelites gave tithes of their annual incomes. Their tasks differed from those of the warriors, but they formed with them one united nation, and were always numbered among the tribes of Israel.

At the present time, all the people of God have access equally to the holy place of prayer and communion. Different duties may be assigned, but all the followers of Christ are at the same time warriors and worshipers. If some serve in the preaching of the word or in the administering of sacraments, they should not form a distinct caste. They should not be regarded as belonging to a priestly tribe. If they are exempt from some duties, if they are appointed to some specific forms of work, it is only as servants of their fellow worshipers. All are enrolled alike in the hosts of the redeemed. Those who belong to Christ share the privilege of serving Him in various places and capacities; all rejoice that their "names are written in heaven"; all trust that they are registered in "the Lamb's Book of Life."

The *camp* of the Israelites and the *order of march* were arranged with symmetry and care. The central object was the Tabernacle or Tent of Meeting. This was the pavilion of the King, the place of worship, the house of God. Around it the tribes were stationed. The camp was thus a picture and a parable of God's dwelling in the midst of His people.

On the east, nearest the entrance, were pitched

the tents of Moses and of Aaron and his sons. On the other three sides, close to the Tabernacle, the Levites were encamped. At some distance, in four groups of three each, the other tribes were stationed. Each of these four divisions had its appointed commander and its own standard. The separate tribes had their distinguishing ensigns. To the tribe of Judah was assigned the place of honor. It was on the east of the Tabernacle, and with it were encamped the tribes of Issachar and Zebulun. On the south was "the standard of the camp of Reuben"; the associated tribes were Simeon and Gad. To the west, under the leadership of Ephraim, were Manasseh and Benjamin. On the north Dan was encamped, together with Asher and Naphtali.

This arrangement of the tribes was not a matter of caprice or of chance. It had a definite reference to their ancestral relationships. These "Children of Israel" (or "Sons of Jacob") were descendants of four mothers. The tribes nearest of kin were placed in the same groups. The eastern camp was composed exclusively of the "sons" of Leah, namely Judah, Issachar, and Zebulun. In the southern corps were the two remaining "sons" of Leah, with the tribe of Gad, the descendants of her handmaid Zilpah. On the west all were descendants of Rachel. On the north were the descendants of Rachel's adopted sons, and of their half-brother Asher.

It is to be noted that after the conquest of Caanan the division of the land among the tribes had regard to these family relationships. Issachar and Zebulun had adjoining territories. Reuben and Gad were together on the east of the Jordan. Benjamin, Ephraim and Manasseh were closely united, and Asher adjoined Naphtali.

When the camp was moved, the *order of march* observed the same divisions of the tribes. First of all came Judah with Issachar and Zebulun; then the Tabernacle, carried in various parts by certain families of Levites; then the division of Reuben, followed by the Levites, who bore the furniture of the Sacred Tent. Lastly came the divisions of Ephraim and of Dan.

Each tribe was under the command of an appointed leader. In every case this was the prince who had assisted in numbering the people. The Supreme Commander, however, was Jehovah their God. Whether in the encampment or on the march, the Tabernacle, the visible symbol of His presence, was in the midst of the hosts. All of His people equally were dependent upon him. To him all had access. So likewise, when at last Canaan had been conquered, and Jerusalem had become the glorious capital, it could be said of the Holy City: "God is in the midst of her, she shall not be moved."

So, too, for every city and nation, real security, true prosperity and peace, depend upon the recognition of the presence and power of God and upon obedience to His laws.

This picture of the tribes of Israel grouped around the Tent of Meeting must have been in the thought of the "Beloved Disciple," when, in prophetic vision, he saw "a new heaven and a new earth," and caught a glimpse of the nations which at last would realize the divine purpose and rejoice in the light of the New Jerusalem. He "heard a great voice out of heaven saying: "Behold the tabernacle of God is with men, and he will dwell with them, and they shall be his peoples, and God himself shall be with them and be their God" (Rev. 21:1-3. R.V.).

It is a Christian belief that in the divine economy every individual has a given place and an allotted task. Such a providence is pictured in this book of the Bible which recounts the "numbering" of Israel. This census was not only a record of the numerical strength of each tribe (Ch. 1) or the battle array of the warriors, whether encamped or on the march, (Ch. 2), but was also an account of the specific duties assigned to the families of *Levi,* the tribe which was exempt from military service and devoted wholly to religious duties connected with the Tabernacle (Chs. 3, 4).

Of these families there were three. They were the sons of Gershon, of Kohath and of Merari. The most prominent were the *Kohathites,* for to this family belonged Moses and Aaron. The first of these brothers was divinely prepared and commissioned to be the leader, the deliverer and the lawgiver of Israel. The work assigned to him was unparalleled in the history of his race.

To Aaron and his sons was assigned the sacred office of the priesthood. All the important functions of this office are described in the Book of Leviticus, which is a handbook for worship. So holy was this calling that any other Israelite who intruded upon its ceremonies or assumed its privileges was smitten with death. Indeed, the two elder sons of Aaron, namely Nadab and Abihu, for a rash disregard of the ceremonial law, forfeited their lives.

While Moses, as commander-in-chief, and Aaron the high priest and his sons were stationed to the east, all other Kohathites encamped on the south side of the Tabernacle; and its sacred furniture was entrusted to their care whenever the camp was moved.

The *sons of Gershon* were stationed on the west. They were commissioned to carry all the "hangings" when the location of the Tabernacle was being changed. These would include the curtains of "fine linen," the cloth of goats' hair, the coverings of rams' skins and of badgers' skins, the curtains of the sanctuary and the court, with the exception of the "veil," which was wrapped around the ark. To aid them in this task they were provided with two wagons and four oxen (Ch. 7:7).

In such transportation of the Tabernacle, the heaviest burdens were assigned to the *Merarites,* who encamped on the north side of the Tabernacle. To them were given four wagons and eight oxen, as they were allotted the solid parts of the Tent and its court, including the framework of "boards" and the "bars" and the pillars and sockets of the court.

When in preparation for the march the Tabernacle was to be taken down, the greatest care was exercised in guarding its sacred parts, and in making them ready for the wilderness journey. As only the priests could enter the holy Tent, Aaron and his sons covered the ark with the "veil," then with a protection of badgers' skins, and then with a cloth of blue. Like-

wise, a blue cloth was used to cover the table of shew-
bread. Over its contents and dishes were placed a
scarlet cloth, and then a covering of badgers' skins.
In the same way, the "golden candlestick" with its
vessels was covered, and was then placed on a frame.
The golden altar was similarly covered. Lastly, the
altar of brass, cleansed of ashes, was covered with
purple, then with badgers' skins, and, as was true of
the golden altar and the "table," staves were inserted
in the rings so that it could be carried on the shoulders of the Levites. Until all was ready the Levites
were not allowed to come near, but now they ap-
proached and undertook the burdens which had been
assigned to each family and to each individual.

Such a picture of the hosts of Israel encamped
around the Tabernacle, the central place of worship,
which was closely encircled by the tents of the Levites, the ministers of worship, gives the impression
of a people who belonged to God, and it belongs to
a book of religion quite as much as to a chapter of
history.

This impression of the sacred character of Israel
is deepened by what is here recorded further concerning *the tribe of Levi* (Ch. 3:40-51). Its members
were granted not to Moses the military chieftain, but
to Aaron the High Priest and to his sons as a gift, to
aid these priests in their sacred tasks. What is even
more significant, they were representatives of the
whole nation in their daily worship of God. As God
had delivered the first-born of the Israelites on the
night of the Passover, when the first-born of the
Egyptians perished, He claimed as His own special

possession the first-born of His people. However, He appointed to sacred service in their place all the members of the tribe of Levi. Therefore, the Levites served in the place of all the first-born of Israel. Thus we have a nation prepared not so much for conflict or conquest as to stand among the people of the earth as a witness to the power and grace of the one living and true God.

When the numbering was made it was discovered that the first-born among the tribes exceeded the number of Levites by two hundred and seventy-three. Since for these there was none to take their places in the holy service of the Tabernacle, they were "redeemed" by the payment of five shekels apiece, which money was given to Aaron and his sons.

Such an arbitrary method of redemption is contrasted by the Apostle Peter with the redemption secured by Christ for His followers: "Ye were redeemed not with corruptible things, with silver and gold from your vain manner of life handed down from your fathers, but with the precious blood of Christ as of a lamb, without blemish and without spot" (I Peter 1:18). The contrast here is not only with the price but also with the purpose of redemption. Christ gave Himself for us, not that we might be exempt from forms of sacred service which God might have required from us, but that in all our lives and with all our powers we might be consecrated to Him as "an holy priesthood to offer up spiritual sacrifices acceptable to God by Jesus Christ."

## The Consecration of the Army [Chs. 5, 6]

As each one of the Israelites had an appointed task, so too each one was expected to obey God and to be submissive to His will. It was no ordinary army which had been organized, but a holy people consecrated to God.

In holiness and consecration the essential idea is that of separation, more definitely of separation from sin and separation for service. Therefore, when the hosts had been numbered, the next step in preparation for the march consisted in the purification of the camp (Ch. 5:1-4).

Lepers and persons otherwise diseased were excluded, and also those who had come in contact with the dead. In part the purpose was to prevent contagion; yet it was not only a sanitary precaution but also a ceremonial prohibition. Those excluded were not regarded as sinful but as disqualified from partaking in public worship. Furthermore, the law may be regarded as symbolic and as typifying the truth that sin makes fellowship with God impossible.

There were also moral faults which must be corrected for the further purification of the camp. All guilty of trespasses against their fellow Israelites must confess and must make restitution. It will be remembered that "trespasses" constituted a particular class of sins, namely, those which consisted in invading the property rights of other persons. These included theft, withholding of wages, fraud in a bargain or in the treatment of a deposit, dishonest retaining of an article which had been found, and combining false swearing with any of these offenses. Such practices could not be tolerated in the camp of a holy army. Full restitution must be made and one-fifth of the amount involved must be offered. In case the injured person had died, the restitution must be made to a relative, or if such could not be found, then the payment must be made to the priest. If such requirements were made in the camp of Israel how much more should they be enforced in the church of Christ (vs. 5-10).

The purity of the camp also was safeguarded against sins of a more serious character, notably against infidelity in the marriage relation.

If a wife, even though innocent of fault, was under suspicion, she was subject to a most terrifying ordeal. She was brought to the priest in the sanctuary and made to sit in the presence of the Lord with her hair loose and disheveled, holding in her hands a meager offering of unscented barley meal. Water was taken from the sacred laver and in it was placed dust from the floor of the Tabernacle. The priest pronounced an oath embodying a frightful curse in case the woman was guilty; and to this she responded, "Amen, amen." The oath was written on a scroll or tablet and then washed in the "bitter water," so that to drink the water was to be identified with the oath in full acceptance. The meal offering was then presented and the woman was made to drink the bitter potion. If she was innocent no ill effect followed, but if guilty the result was deadly and the woman became "a curse among her people." Such an ordeal was seldom if ever inflicted, as far as can be learned; but its legal establishment must have gone far in maintaining the purity of the consecrated hosts of Israel (vs. 11-31).

However, separation from sin is only one aspect of holiness; the more positive form is shown in devotion and consecration to the service of God. The supreme expression of such devotion was found in the *vow of the Nazarite*. The word for "Nazarite," more exactly spelled *"Nazirite,"* indicated separation. It denoted one who was separated, or dedicated to God. The vow was purely voluntary and it usually was taken for a limited time. However, one might be dedicated at birth and always live as a Nazarite. Such was the case with Samson and Samuel and John the Baptist.

The three features of this vow were the following: (1) abstinence from wine, (2) allowing the hair and beard to grow uncut, (3) avoidance of all contact with the dead.

Wine and the products of the vine were supposed to indicate a settled life and were symbols of comfort and enjoyment. The hair was a symbol of physical strength and of dignity. Contact with the dead resulted in ceremonial uncleanness, and in the case of the Nazarite made it impossible to render those services which natural affection might require.

However, the Nazarite was not a hermit or an ascetic. He mingled in society and was usually a man of action. The purpose of his vow was to express his gratitude for some blessing, or to enforce his promise when making a special request. In any case it was designed to indicate complete consecration to God and a readiness to render to Him any possible service which He might require. As a result of such consecration the Nazarite was "filled with the Spirit" of God and granted extraordinary power and wisdom and influence. He might become a military deliverer like Samson, or a prophet like Samuel or a divinely appointed messenger like John the Baptist (Ch. 6:1-8).

If during the time of his vow the Nazarite became ceremonially unclean by an accidental death taking place by his side, he must submit to a ceremony of purification, offer sacrifices for atonement, and count as lost the days of separation already passed. The period of supreme dedication to God must be begun anew (vs. 9-12).

When the period of the vow was limited, the time of its expiration was marked by an elaborate ceremonial which indicated that the vow had expressed a definite relation to God. The Nazarite presented himself to the priest and brought a sin offering to indicate that he had not been free from fault even during the time of his consecration. He also brought a burnt offering as a symbol of the complete consecration which should continue even when the period of the vow had expired. Then, too, there was a peace offering and its accompanying gifts to express gratitude to God and joy in His fellowship (vs. 13-21).

For the followers of Christ the Nazarite gave an example of consecration full of practical significance. One who is wholly devoted to Christ may wish to deny himself certain things which are not sinful, but which may lessen his influence and unfit him for the largest service. The restrictions which he places upon himself may be purely voluntary but may be assumed with definite purpose. It is not enough for a Christian to refrain from practices which society regards as evil, he should be willing to practice self-denial in matters which in themselves may be innocent. One may abstain from the use of wine and alcoholic beverages in view of the intemperance and injury which indulgence makes so widespread. He may refrain from certain forms of amusement which are attended with peril. He may devote his powers and his position to unselfish service which is voluntarily assumed. He may even refuse to do what the most tender ties of relationship may seem to require, when he fears that to yield would be to make him unfit for worship and communion with God. In some sense all Christians should be Nazarites in spirit, and follow in the footsteps of the Master who did not withdraw from human fellowship, yet lived a life of complete self-denial that He might fulfil his divine mission. The history of Nazarites should teach us also that where there is true devotion to God there is always granted a special measure of His Spirit.

Furthermore, consecration always issues in blessing. Thus, after this regulation of the Nazarite Vow, there follows the *Priestly Benediction:*

> The Lord bless thee, and keep thee:
> The Lord make his face to shine upon thee,
>     and be gracious unto thee:
> The Lord lift up his countenance upon thee,
>     and give thee peace (Ch. 6:24-26).

This is rhythmical, musical, poetic. No prayer

more exquisite, more impressive, more comprehensive can be found in the Old Testament or the New. It is in truth "The Lord's Prayer." God gave it to Aaron and his sons to use as an inspired formula. It was to express His acceptance of a people consecrated to His service and to remind them of His promise to grant them His grace.

The benediction is contained in three lines, each consisting of two clauses. Each begins with the sacred name. Each repeats the singular pronoun "thee," as blessings are invoked on Israel collectively as well as on each individual Israelite.

The first petition refers to the providence of God, positively, in the bestowal of His divine favor and benefits, and, negatively, in His protecting care. This idea of God as the Keeper of Israel is familiar and is beautifully expressed in the lines of the 121st Psalm:

The Lord is thy keeper:
The Lord is thy shade upon thy right hand. . . .
The Lord shall preserve thy going out and thy coming in
From this time forth, and even for evermore.

The second line is a prayer that the Lord will "make his face to shine," that is, "will regard with his approving smile," and will "be gracious" in showing proofs of His special favor.

The hymn rises in a grand crescendo until it culminates with the request for the highest gift that God can bestow or man receive, namely, that "peace," that tranquility of heart and life, which results when God lifts His "countenance" upon one with divine sympathy and love.

Thus, by this threefold repetition, the priest would "put" the sacred "name upon the children of Israel" as the seal of their acceptance and the source of their blessing (Ch. 6:27).

## THE OFFERING OF THE PRINCES [Ch. 7]

Consecration to God may be expressed not only in moral purity (Ch. 5) or in self-denial with a view to service (Ch. 6), but also in the support of public worship (Ch. 7). Thus after the cleansing of the congregation and the regulation of the "Nazarite Vow" there follows the account of the gifts made by the tribal chieftains for the service of the Tabernacle. Each tribe was represented by the prince who had been named in the numbering of the people and had assisted with this census (Ch. 1).

Their gifts consisted, first of all, in "six covered wagons, and twelve oxen; a wagon for two of the princes, and for each one an ox." This was to provide for the transporting of the Tabernacle whenever the camp was moved. "Two wagons and four oxen" were given to "the sons of Gershon," to whom were entrusted all the curtains and hangings of the sacred structure. "Four wagons and eight oxen" were provided for "the sons of Merari," whose task it was to transport the boards and beams and heavier portions of the sanctuary. None was given to "the sons of Kobath," for they were expected to carry on their shoulders the articles of furniture, such as the ark, the "table," the "candlestick" and the altars, which were too holy to be otherwise conveyed.

At the time when the Tabernacle service was inaugurated the twelve princes, each on a separate day, presented offerings to be used in the prescribed forms of worship. These offerings were identical in all cases. They were enumerated as follows: a silver "charger" and a "silver bowl," both filled with "fine flour mingled with oil"; a "golden spoon . . . filled with incense"; a bullock, "a lamb for a burnt offering," a kid, "two oxen, five rams, five he goats, five lambs."

Over and over again the exact list is repeated, each time with the name of the prince who represented one of the twelve tribes of Israel. The accounting occupies eighty-nine verses, forming one of the longest chapters of the Bible. The iteration may appear monotonous and prolix, yet it is rather impressive, and indicates the reverence for the Tabernacle worship which must have been awakened in the minds of the people, as, day after day during those twelve long days, they saw the processions moving from the various camps led by the chief princes of the nation and bearing the rich gifts for the service of God.

This list may make its impression on the people of God today. It intimates that they should be eager to bring their free-will offerings for the support of divine worship. Each gift is recorded, and in the sight of the Lord all are equal where there is equal devotion and reverence and love.

The long chapter closes with a statement which

should encourage such offerings. When the gifts had been presented there came in response a divine message through Moses, as when provision is made for worship there is sure to follow some new revelation of the presence and power and grace of God:

And when Moses was gone into the tabernacle of the congregation to speak with him [that is, with God], then he heard the voice of one speaking unto him from off the mercy seat that was upon the ark of testimony, from between the two cherubims: and he [that is God] spake unto him (Ch. 7:89).

## THE ORDINATION OF THE LEVITES [Ch. 8]

In the Holy of Holies the voice of God had been heard as He graciously accepted the generous gifts of the princes. The thought is turned next to the Holy Place, where, for the first time, the sacred lamps were lighted; and then to the court of the Tabernacle, where the Levites, when consecrated, were to render their appointed service.

The *Golden Candlestick*, or more properly the Golden Lampstand, stood on the south side of the Holy Place, and lighted this first of the two curtained rooms which constituted the "Tent of Meeting." Its seven branches ended in lamps filled with oil. This beautiful piece of furniture is an accepted symbol of the people of God, whether ancient Israel (Zech. 4) or the churches of the New Testament (Rev. 1:20). When filled with His Spirit, of which oil was the symbol, they could perform their intended function, and by their witness to their Lord, could shine as lights in the world.

The mention of this candlestick just here has been regarded as a strange interruption of the story which relates the gifts for the Tabernacle and then the consecration of the Levites; but this was the exact order of the events, and, furthermore, it has been regarded as bearing a symbolic message. Only in the light of the Holy Place can gifts of princes or service of Levites appear in their real value. Their worth is manifest only as they are shown to glorify God.

As to *the ordination,* its essential features were, first of all, the cleansing, which consisted in being sprinkled with water, in shaving the body and washing the clothes, typifying the moral purity of those who bore the vessels of the Lord; and, second, in sacrificing one bullock as a sin offering and another as a burnt offering; and, third, in publicly presenting the Levites to Aaron and his sons to assist them in their sacred ministries. These Levites were said to take the place of the first-born, who, in turn, represented the various families of Israel. Thus they served in the place and in the name of the whole congregation. So in performing the services which were due from all the people, and which if omitted would occasion the displeasure of God, the Levites were said "to make atonement for the children of Israel." This substitution in place of the first-born was regarded as a mercy on the part of God; for if the first-born had been expected to perform in person the sacred tasks of the sanctuary, they might have failed, or have rendered such imperfect service as to draw down some divine penalty; or, as the historian states, "that there be no plague among the children of Israel" (v. 19).

These truths as to mediation and substitution run through the entire course of Scripture and find their climax in the atoning work of Christ, our Great High Priest.

The fact that the Levites relieved the people from certain forms of ritual observance did not relieve the latter from their appointed service in the armies of Israel. So the acceptance of Christ as our representative in His saving ministry obligates us to undertake our daily tasks with more eagerness and to show ourselves worthy to be regarded as belonging to Him who loved us and gave Himself for us.

The service of Levites was limited to the years from twenty-five to fifty. Later on, in some cases, from twenty or from thirty years, and certain tasks could be performed by those of more advanced age. It is needless to remark that one enlists in the service of Christ for life, yes, for time and for eternity.


## THE SECOND PASSOVER [Ch. 9:1-14]

The Feast of Passover was the type and counterpart of the Sacred Supper of our Lord. Each points backward to a past deliverance and forward to a greater deliverance to come. Passover commemorated the rescue of Israel from bondage in Egypt and looked forward to the redemption of the world to be wrought by Christ. The Sacrament recalls the redeeming death of our Lord and looks forward to the completed salvation to be accomplished when He comes again.

A year has passed since that night when the Israelites had observed the Paschal Feast, when the angel of death had "passed over" their homes, and when, in haste, they were led forth from the land of bondage. Now they had crossed the desert as far as Sinai. There they had received the Law, and made a covenant with God to be His people. They were about to be organized into an army, and to begin their march toward the Land of Promise, when the command came to them to observe the Passover according to the previous direction of God. This they did "in the first month of the second year after they were come out of the land of Egypt" (Ch. 9:1). Therefore, this second historic passover was observed before the "numbering" of the people, which has given to this book its name (Ch. 1:1). However, it is recorded here because there may have existed an uncertainty as to whether the feast should be observed in the wilderness before reaching Canaan, and also because an occasion had arisen for further instruction as to the Passover. This occasion was the question raised by "certain men who were defiled by the dead body of a man" as to whether or not they should partake of the Passover feast. If they did not partake they would be neglecting a sacred duty; if they did partake when unclean they would be guilty of grievous sacrilege. What should they do? They consulted Moses, and Moses consulted God. The result was the divine direction for establishing a supplementary feast, often called the "Little Passover."

According to this provision, one who was unclean might be purified, or one who had been absent on a long journey, might observe the Passover one month later than the day prescribed by the law.

This provision, however, could not be regarded as an excuse for carelessly neglecting the feast of "the fourteenth day of the first month," nor could any of the exact requirements of the ceremonial be omitted. It was purely a provision for accidental circumstances and for conditions beyond one's control. The ordinance was enforced by most solemn sanctions.

Furthermore, it was enacted that people of other races who accepted all the laws and customs of the Israelites might unite with them in such acts of sacred worship.

It would be impossible to avoid certain serious warnings which the narrative contains for any Christians who willfully neglect the Lord's Supper, or who are careless in its observance.

"This do in remembrance of me" is not casual advice, but the explicit command of our divine Master; yet no one should approach His table without due repentance and the cleansing which the Saviour is ready to provide. He knows how much we need the strength and encouragement which communion with Him and with one another supply as we continue on our wilderness journey; and He reminds us that "the stranger" of every race and land belongs to the one Body in which are numbered all who truly trust in Christ.

## THE CLOUD AND THE TRUMPETS
### [Ch. 9:15 to 10:10]

To the people of God no symbol of divine guidance has been more precious and more significant than that of the "pillar of cloud and of fire." This luminous object rested on the Tabernacle. It furnished light by night and shade by day. The Israelites regarded it as the chariot of their Commander, the pavilion of their King. Whenever the cloud moved they understood that their armies were to go forward; where the cloud rested they encamped and there the hosts remained, "whether it were two days of a month, or a year."

What the exact nature of this *"pillar of fire"* was it is useless to conjecture. Evidently it was God's instrument for guiding His people. It was for them the symbol of His continual presence. When they encamped He was in their midst. When they moved forward He led the way. He was ever their Leader, their Protector, their Support. No doubt Moses and his followers were expected to exercise their reason and their judgment, and to secure knowledge and advice from natural and human sources, but through all the wilderness journey their dependence was on the Lord. On the other hand, they were expected to be submissive to His will and obedient to His command.

So, for the followers of Christ, life is a journey through a land of mysteries toward the "better country," and all the way they are assured of the presence of their Lord. He guides them on their way. He marks for them the stages of the journey. They see no visible "pillar of fire" but they have the divine promise: "Lo, I am with you alway." The method of His guidance may be veiled in mystery, but in the experience of His people it is a glorious reality. They must use their powers and consider His providences yet ever be ready to trust and obey. They must be active and resolute but must follow His guidance and depend on His grace. At times the hosts of the Lord must be patient and wait for the moving of the cloud.

However, the cloud was not the only means by which the commands of the Leader were communicated to His followers. There was also the sounding of the *"Silver Trumpets."* These were two in number and their various notes formed a definite code which all the people could understand. If both trumpets were blown the congregation assembled at the door of the Tabernacle; if only one, the princes would gather to meet with Moses. When there was a protracted peal, an "alarm," it was a signal for breaking camp and beginning the march. This last purpose is the reason why the silver trumpets are mentioned here. It is an indication that the preparations which have been recorded in the preceding chapters of the book have been completed, and the army is now ready to move forward.

However, other uses for these trumpets were to be made in future years. They could be blown as a call to war, or to announce the observance of the glad feasts and festivals of the sacred year.

The sounding of the Silver Trumpets was symbolic of the voice of God. The cloud might direct the moving tribes, but the trumpet spoke to each and every member of the host. So there is a real sense in which God makes His will known to each one of his people. He speaks by His Spirit and His word. He also employs human reason and conscience and divine providence to make plain His will. There must be an attentive ear and a submissive mind, and then it is certain the voice of the Lord will be heard. He will tell us when to rest and when to journey, when to prepare for conflict, and when to enjoy the gladness of the sacred feasts and the holy convocations. Those who have learned to listen for His voice are ready for the daily journey and for the tasks of each hour.

## II

## *THE WANDERINGS IN THE WILDERNESS*

NUMBERS 10:11 to 19:22

### The Departure from Sinai [Ch. 10:11-36]

Thus the journey was begun,—under the guiding cloud, at the sound of the silver trumpets, with standards raised and banners unfurled, each tribe in its appointed place. First came the three tribes under the standard of Judah, followed by the Levites, who carried the curtains and hangings and the framework of the Tabernacle. Then came the tribes of Reuben, Simeon, and Gad, protecting the Levites who were entrusted with the ark, the altars, and other sacred furniture. Six tribes came next, leading the hosts of camp followers and herds of cattle. Thus the ark was ever in the van, and even though not in the front line of battle, as some insist, it could be regarded as "leading" the armies, as it was the most sacred of all visible objects and was regarded as the throne of the King; and where it rested marked the place of encampment.

The guidance of cloud and trumpets, and the movement of the ark, did not make superfluous the aid of human knowledge or the exercise of human judgment. Thus Moses urged Hobab, his father-in-law (or "brother-in-law") to accompany him on the journey. The home of this "Kenite" was in the very regions through which the tribes were passing. His familiarity with the places of pasture, the location of wells and springs, and with the possibilities of attacks, would be invaluable. The cloud could mark the general direction; one like Hobab could supply the needed information as to particular situations and conditions.

Moses has been criticised for not relying wholly on the guidance of God; but divine guidance should ever be associated with human effort and the exercise of reason.

Hobab hesitated at first, but seems to have yielded subsequently to the appeals of his kinsman, and ultimately to have reached the land of promise (Judges 1:16, 4:11; I Sam. 15:6).

The invitation extended by Moses to Hobab was in terms so beautiful and full of meaning that it often should be on the lips of the followers of Christ and be addressed by them to their kindred and friends:

We are journeying unto the place of which the Lord said, I will give it you; come thou with us, and we will do thee good: for the Lord hath spoken good concerning Israel.

However much Moses desired human help and counsel, his confidence was ever in the presence and power of God. To him every stage of the journey was a divine achievement. It was begun with a majestic prayer, and concluded with a similar solemn petition. His invitation to Hobab was beautiful, but his prayers to God were to be re-echoed in the Psalms of Israel through all the coming centuries:

And it came to pass, when the ark set forward, that Moses said, Rise up, Lord, and let thine enemies be scattered: and let them that hate thee flee before thee. And when it rested, he said, Return, O Lord, unto the many thousands of Israel.

## THE SIN OF DISCONTENT [Ch. 11]

Murmuring and discontent are not uncommon even among the people of God who have heard His voice and been under the guidance of the "cloud." Conditions often are so distressing that to complain may seem natural, but it is always a fault. The Israelites had only started on the wilderness journey when they became discouraged by their burdens, and by the heat and discomfort and weariness of the way. "And when the people complained, it displeased the Lord: and the Lord heard it; and his anger was kindled; and the fire of the Lord burnt among them, and consumed them that were in the uttermost parts of the camp. And the people cried unto Moses; and when Moses prayed unto the Lord, the fire was quenched."

Even so severe a penalty did not dispel the spirit of discontent. "The mixed multitude [partly Egyptians] that was among them fell a lusting [longing for other kinds of food]: and the children of Israel also wept again, and said, Who shall give us flesh to eat? We remember the fish, which we did eat in Egypt freely; the cucumbers, and the melons, and the leeks and the onions, and the garlick; but now our soul is dried away: there is nothing at all, beside this manna, before our eyes" (vs. 4-6). They remembered the fish and the fruits of Egypt; they seem to have forgotten the brick kilns, the burdens and the sting of the taskmaster's lash. They were mindful of their discomfort but forgetful of the God who was guiding them and supplying the manna which was sufficient for their daily food.

"Then Moses heard the people weep throughout their families, every man in the door of his tent: and the anger of the Lord was kindled greatly; Moses also was displeased." The effect on Moses was pitiful. The people had yielded to discontent, but Moses gave himself over to absolute despair: "And Moses said unto the Lord, Wherefore hast thou afflicted thy servant? and wherefore have I not found favour in thy sight, that thou layest the burden of all this people upon me? . . . I am not able to bear all this people alone, because it is too heavy for me. And if thou deal thus with me, kill me, I pray thee, out of hand, if I have found favour in thy sight; and let me not see my wretchedness."

Moses was taking himself too seriously. There is always a point beyond which even a parent or a ruler is not responsible for the failures and faults of others. Then, again, the "burden" was not laid on Moses alone. Surely God was sharing its weight. Furthermore, even when one fails in his task, he should not ask to die. There is always something else to be done by one for God and for his fellow men.

God comforted His despondent servant by appointing seventy "elders" who would share with Moses the cares of leadership. He answered the cry of the people by the promise of an oversupply of the flesh they craved.

When the "seventy elders" gathered at the door of the Tabernacle the Spirit of God came upon them and they all prophesied. They did not predict future events, but they gave ecstatic utterances in praise of God. When it is stated that "they did not cease," the translation might be "they did so no more." The idea is that the gift of "prophecy" was temporary; it authenticated their appointment as "rulers." The Spirit of God would still give them power for their duties, even though they did not speak as "prophets."

Two men of the "seventy," Eldad and Medad, were not with the others at the door of the Tabernacle; but they began to prophesy "in the camp." Such a divine gift is not limited by localities. However, when the report of their prophesying was brought to Moses, he was urged by Joshua to forbid them. Joshua seemed to fear that some of his prestige might be lost by Moses, and that all powers of leadership needed to be concentrated in one place. The reply of Moses indicated his broad-minded and unselfish tolerance: "And Moses said unto him, Enviest thou for my sake? would God that all the Lord's people were prophets, and that the Lord would put his spirit upon them!"

As for the promise to the people, a southeast wind brought flocks of quail from the neighborhood of the Red Sea, where quail abounded. Wearied by their flight, the birds moved in great numbers near the ground and were easily taken by the Israelites. The quail were killed and spread out to dry in the sun. For many days the people indulged in a surfeit of this rich but dangerous food, until they were smitten "with a very great plague." The Lord has used the answer to their prayers as an instrument for their punishment and rebuke. They came to look with loathing upon the very flesh for which they had yearned. The name of the place significantly was called "Kibroth-hattaavah," that is, "the graves of lust."

"Now these things were our examples," writes the apostle, "to the intent we should not lust after evil things as they also lusted. . . . Neither murmur ye, as some of them also murmured and were destroyed of the destroyer" (I Cor. 10:6, 9).

Paul himself knew what it was to be weary and hungry and in physical distress; he had experienced all the hardships of the wilderness journey; but he pressed forward with triumphant courage; he reached a place where he could say: "I have learned, in whatsoever state I am, therewith to be content" (Phil. 4:11).

## THE JEALOUSY OF MIRIAM [Ch. 12]

That was a celebrated family circle which consisted of Moses and Aaron and Miriam. They were regarded as the divinely given leaders and deliverers of their nation. As Micah states, "I brought thee up out of the land of Egypt, and redeemed thee out of the house of servants; and I sent before thee Moses,

Aaron and Miriam" (Micah 6:4). They represent three chief factors of human society. Moses is the embodiment of law and government, Aaron represents religion, and Miriam is the exponent of art. Yet they were all related to religious faith. The laws enunciated by Moses were the laws which had been communicated by God. Aaron gave the people a liturgy which was symbolic and of divine origin. Miriam was a poetess and a musician whose art was dedicated wholly to divine service.

The life of Miriam is sketched in three impressive scenes. When she first appears she is standing on the banks of the Nile, concerned with the safety of her little brother Moses. The boy had been born at a time when the king of Egypt had decreed the death of every male infant. For three months Moses had been concealed by his parents. Then his mother adopted a desperate expedient, or rather she exhibited a surprising act of faith. She put the babe in a little ark of bulrushes and placed it among the flags by the river's brink at the place where the Egyptian princess was accustomed to bathe. When the daughter of Pharaoh spied the beautiful child, quick-witted Miriam stepped forth with the proposal, "Shall I go call to thee a nurse of the Hebrew women that she may nurse the child for thee?" She acted with marvelous promptness but also with consummate wisdom when she brought to the princess the mother of the babe without intimating the relationship, which disclosure might have caused the whole plan to fail. The babe is adopted by the princess as her son, and it is Miriam who has saved the life of a child who became the deliverer of the nation from which came the Saviour of the world.

In the second scene Miriam is standing by the shores of the Red Sea. Israel has escaped from Egyptian bondage but has been pursued by Pharaoh and his hosts. However, the Egyptians have been engulfed in the waters of the sea, and in the morning the Israelites are standing in safety on the farther side of the waters. It is then that Miriam comes forward with her timbrel and her song. She teaches the choirs of women to sing the song of triumph accompanied by a sacred dance and by the sound of timbrels: "Sing ye to the Lord, for he hath triumphed gloriously; the horse and his rider hath he thrown into the sea." Miriam appears as the worthy representative of those noble women who through the ages have used the gift of sacred song to lead in the praise of God and to encourage His people on their wilderness journey toward the promised land.

In the third scene Miriam is standing, not by the bank of the Nile or on the shore of the Red Sea, but is hiding in shame behind the sand hills of the desert. She has become a despised leper, driven out of the camp of Israel in misery and in disgrace. She is suffering the penalty of a grievous fault. She had become the victim of the most cruel and common passion which assails the human soul. She had grown envious of the supreme power and position of Moses. She had grown bitter and had made a heartless and traitorous attack on her brother. She had even implicated Aaron in her disloyalty. Poor Aaron, weak and pliable, previously had been persuaded by the people to lead them in the worship of a golden calf, and then had stood by Miriam when she passionately reproached the divinely appointed leader of Israel. The occasion of her outburst of anger was the marriage of Moses to a Cushite or Ethiopian woman. In such a marriage there was nothing contrary to law or custom. Evidently the wife whom Moses had married forty years before was dead. There was only one reason for objecting to the step which Moses had taken. The anger of Miriam was due to her jealousy. There are those who defend her attitude of mind and her course of action. They insist that she was moved purely by love of her people. She feared that a woman of another race might lead Moses into some disloyalty to God. Such an attempted defense seems futile. The narrative makes it quite plain that Miriam, and not Moses, was seriously at fault. It is not difficult to imagine why Miriam had become envious. For long years she had occupied with Moses the place of leadership, of power and of comradeship. She was the supreme woman of Israel. It was difficult for her to be supplanted, to become in any sense subordinate, even to have Moses share his affection with another. She appears in the presence of Moses declaring that she and Aaron are at least his equals, even in the rôle of prophets, "and they said, Hath the Lord indeed spoken only by Moses? Hath he not spoken also by us?"

"And the Lord heard it." Moses likewise must have heard it, but he makes no reply, and the historian significantly adds, "Now the man Moses was very meek, above all the men which were upon the face of the earth." He may have been offended; he even may have been angered, but he makes no endeavor to defend himself or to claim his superior commission; but "the Lord heard it." "And the Lord spake suddenly unto Moses, and unto Aaron, and unto Miriam, Come out ye three unto the tabernacle of the congregation. And they three came out. And the Lord came down in the pillar of the cloud, and stood in the door of the tabernacle, and called Aaron and Miriam: and they both came forth. And he said, Hear now my words: If there be a prophet among you, I the Lord will make myself known unto him in a vision, and will speak unto him in a dream. My servant Moses is not so, who is faithful in all mine house. With him will I speak mouth to mouth, even apparently, and not in dark speeches; and the similitude of the Lord shall he behold: wherefore then were ye not afraid to speak against my servant Moses?" Thus the Lord sets forth the supreme and unparalleled position of Moses as His appointed mouth piece and prophet. He might speak through others by visions and dreams, but to Moses, His faithful servant, He would speak directly and clearly, and to Moses He would give a unique revelation of His divine person and power and grace. One who spoke against Moses, therefore, would be speaking against God. The grievous fault of Miriam and Aaron was, therefore, that of disloyalty to God and treason against His established government.

This is the real character of jealousy. It is in a true sense rebellion against the Most High. When we remember that talents and position and power are granted in the providence of God, it is real rebellion against His will to be envious of those to whom these powers or privileges have been assigned.

The penalty visited upon Miriam was severe: "And the anger of the Lord was kindled against them; and he departed." The divine displeasure with Aaron is indicated by the withdrawal of the symbol of God's presence: "And the cloud departed from off the tabernacle."

Yet as Miriam had been the speaker and the chief offender, it is recorded, "Behold, Miriam became leprous, white as snow: and Aaron looked upon Miriam, and behold she was leprous." The detection of this dread disease had been assigned only a short time before to Aaron as the high priest of the nation. What more pitiful penalty could have fallen upon him than to be the one who was to declare his sister not only guilty of a grievous fault but so diseased and repulsive that she must be driven out of the camp, that she must wander in the wilderness, that on the approach of any other person she must cry "Unclean, unclean," and must suffer a lingering and loathsome death.

It is now that Aaron becomes the speaker. He fully recognizes his own fault. He knew something of the anguish of soul which must be felt by one who is compelled to sentence and to punish a partner in crime. He cries out to Moses for pity, "Alas, my lord, I beseech thee, lay not the sin upon us, wherein we have done foolishly, and wherein we have sinned. Let her not be as one dead, of whom the flesh is half consumed." Thus he confesses his own fault and pleads that the punishment due to their sin may not be inflicted. Now for the first time Moses is heard to speak. In his meekness he has made no complaint. He has offered no rebuke, but his heart must have been filled with distress. Now he shows the very spirit which animated our Saviour. He pleads for those who have assailed him, despised him, abused him: "And Moses cried unto the Lord, saying, Heal her now, O God, I beseech thee." Thus the one who has been offended becomes the intercessor.

There is a solemn lesson in the divine reply. God is to forgive and to heal, but first there must be a period and a proof of sincere repentance. Miriam must act as one who realizes her disgrace and her shame: "And the Lord said unto Moses, If her father had but spit in her face, should she not be ashamed seven days? Let her be shut out from the camp seven days, and after that let her be received in again." She was forgiven and restored but she was never the same woman again. Within a year her life is ended and probably those are correct who conjecture that she died of a broken heart.

The message of this sad story intimates to us the pitiful and devastating character of the passion of envy, but also reveals to us the possibility of generous pardon and forgiveness such as that manifested by Moses. It is probably true that jealousy is the most common of human passions and that it has in it no reward, no gratification, no promise. It is as "cruel as death." It was this which made a murderer of one of the first two children in the world. Why did Cain kill his brother? It was envy.

Why did Joseph suffer so cruelly at the hands of his brothers? It was because of their envy. Why was our Saviour delivered to the Romans and nailed to a cross? We read that "it was for envy that they did it." May we be reminded and warned of the peril which lurks in this passion. On the other hand, may we be assured that love can meet the assaults of this enemy. "Love suffereth long and is kind, love envieth not." Then, too, we know that there is an Intercessor ready to forgive us and to plead for our pardon and our deliverance. "He is able to save unto the uttermost those who come unto God by him."

## UNBELIEF AND DEFEAT [Chs. 13, 14]

After leaving Sinai only a brief time had been required for the Israelites to reach the southern border of Canaan, but forty years passed before the people entered the Promised Land. The inspired explanation is as solemn as it is brief: "They could not enter in because of unbelief" (Heb. 3:19).

Even on the short journey they had shown a spirit of disloyalty and rebellion. This spirit was soon to result in national disaster. However, it is not necessary to suppose that unbelief was the motive for sending spies to investigate the land. Many readers so imagine. They conclude that the people, fearing to undertake the conquest of Canaan, asked a delay until the country had been visited by scouts, thus hiding their cowardice under a plea which would postpone action.

Those who so interpret the event do offer a serious and important lesson. They remind us that when we stand at the threshold of a great opportunity we are tempted to fear for the future, and we ask for further light, and we seek to be assured of what awaits us, when in reality we do not need more information but more faith.

It is true that the people were lacking in courage, and also that they had come to Moses with the request that spies should be sent to "search out the land"; but the proposal "pleased" Moses, that inspired, fearless, mouthpiece of God; and the mission was undertaken not only with divine sanction, but by divine command (Deut. 1:22, 23). "And the Lord spake unto Moses, saying, Send thou men, that they may search the land of Canaan, which I give unto the children of Israel: of every tribe of their fathers shall ye send a man, every one a ruler among them" (Ch. 13:1, 2).

This sending of spies was a wise precaution. God does not approve of rashness or presumption. Prudence is not inconsistent with trust in divine providence. A knowledge of the country to be conquered would make possible a wise strategy. It would encourage faith and condemn unbelief. In later years, one of these spies, Joshua, used his knowledge of the land in carrying out his brilliant campaigns and completing the conquest of Canaan.

In dispatching the messengers, Moses laid stress on the two essential facts to be learned, first, the value of the land, and, second, the strength of the inhabitants: "And Moses sent them to spy out the land of Canaan, and said unto them, Get you up this way southward, and go up into the mountain: and see the land, what it is; and the people that dwelleth therein, whether they be strong or weak, few or many; and what the land is that they dwell in, whether it be good or bad; and what cities they be that they dwell in, whether in tents, or in strong holds: and what the land is, whether it be fat or lean, whether there be wood therein, or not. And be ye of good courage, and bring the fruit of the land" (Ch. 13:17-20).

The mission of the spies was carried out with promptness and fidelity. In the space of forty days the whole country was traversed, from the wilderness in the south to Hamath in the extreme north, from the hill country to the valley of the Jordan and to the coasts of the Great Sea. As for "the fruit of the land," they brought as a sample one cluster of grapes, borne on a staff between two men, and also pomegranates and figs.

In their report to Moses they said, "We came unto the land whither thou sentest us, and surely it floweth with milk and honey; and this is the fruit of it. Nevertheless the people be strong that dwell in the land, and the cities are walled, and very great: and moreover we saw the children of Anak there." The news was all very gratifying until the messengers came to that *nevertheless.* That was the word which struck consternation in the hearts of the hearers. The description of a land flowing with "milk and honey" sounded well and good, "nevertheless" those walled cities and those giants were too dreadful, and the people cried out in terror. Then Caleb, the spy who represented the tribe of Judah, "stilled the people before Moses, and said, Let us go up at once, and possess it; for we are well able to overcome it." However, this brave witness was contradicted and silenced by ten of his fellow messengers. They dwelt only on the dangers, and declared in an exaggeration of terror and fear: "We be not able to go up against the people; for they are stronger than we. . . . The land through which we have gone to search it, is a land that eateth up the inhabitants thereof; and all the people we saw in it are men of a great stature. And there we saw the giants, the sons of Anak, which come of the giants: and we were in our own sight as grasshoppers, and so we were in their sight."

At such a report the whole camp of Israel was swept by a frenzy of terror. "And all the congregation lifted up their voice, and cried; and the people wept that night. And all the people of Israel murmured against Moses and against Aaron: and the whole congregation said unto them, Would God that we had died in the land of Egypt! or would God that we had died in this wilderness!"

Nor were they content with blaming Moses and Aaron. They insolently charged God with planning to bring them into a land of destruction and a place of death: "And wherefore hath the Lord brought us unto this land, to fall by the sword, that our wives and our children should be a prey? were it not better for us to return into Egypt? And they said one to another, Let us make a captain, and let us return into Egypt." This was not only mad unbelief but rash rebellion against their divinely appointed leaders and against their King. No wonder that Moses and Aaron in anguish of heart "fell on their faces before all the assembly of the congregation of the children of Israel."

Then it was that Joshua and Caleb made their final impassioned appeal: "The land, which we passed through to search it, is an exceeding good land. If the Lord delight in us, then he will bring us into this land, and give it us; a land which floweth with milk and honey. Only rebel not ye against the Lord, neither fear ye the people of the land; for they are bread for us: their defence is departed from them, and the Lord is with us: fear them not."

Like their ten fellow spies, they had seen the walled cities and the giants, but their message repeated a word which the others had forgotten. These two spies spoke of the *Lord:* "If the Lord delight in us, then he will bring us into this land. Rebel not ye against the Lord; . . . the Lord is with us: fear them not."

"But all the congregation bade stone them with stones." The lives of these loyal leaders might have been forfeit because of their brave testimony; but the Lord intervened. His terrifying presence appeared in the cloud of glory; and the multitude was cowed in silence and fear.

Then the Lord declared to Moses His displeasure: "How long will this people provoke me? and how long will it be ere they believe me, for all the signs which I have shewed among them? I will smite them with the pestilence, and disinherit them, and will make of thee a greater nation and mightier than they." Moses cries out in behalf of the people. His intercession was an act of supreme self-abnegation and of faith. The offer to make of him a great nation in place of the people who were to be destroyed might have been a temptation to a less heroic character. Moses did not think of himself. His intercession expressed only his care for the people and supremely his concern for the honor of God. Indeed, his matchless plea was based wholly on his regard for the name of the Lord and the nature of the Lord.

As Moses argues, the nations had begun to learn something of the saving knowledge of God by His deliverance of Israel from Egypt and by the guidance and protection He had given them in their desert journey. If now Israel is destroyed, this knowledge of God will be lost. "Now if thou shalt kill all this people as one man, then the nations which have heard the fame of thee will speak, saying, Because the Lord was not able to bring this people into the land which he sware unto them, therefore he hath slain them in the wilderness."

So it is today. Every moral failure on the part of a follower of Christ brings discredit on His name and confirms the unbelief of those who may have been inclined to accept the truth of the Gospel.

Moses further argues that God can show His "power" and can reveal further His true nature, not by destroying His people, but by granting them pardon. Such mercy would give to the nations of the world a true conception of the nature of God as already revealed to Israel at Sinai. "And now, I beseech thee, let the power of my Lord be great according as thou hast spoken, saying, The Lord is longsuffering, and of great mercy, forgiving iniquity and transgression, and by no means clearing the guilty, visiting the iniquity of the fathers upon the children unto the third and fourth generation. Pardon, I beseech thee, the iniquity of this people according unto the greatness of thy mercy, and as thou hast forgiven this people, from Egypt even until now."

God replies that He will pardon, but in such a way as will further His purpose of making known in "all the earth" a knowledge of His justice and His mercy. "And the Lord said, I have pardoned according to thy word: but as truly as I live, all the earth shall be filled with the glory of the Lord."

The divine verdict is pronounced. The life of the nation is to be spared. All those who were twenty years of age or younger when they left Egypt are to be pardoned. From them is to come a new people whom God will lead and protect and bring at last into the Land of Promise. As for the rest, they are to wander for forty years in the wilderness, to die for their rebellion, and of them only Joshua and Caleb will enter into Canaan.

When this solemn sentence is reported to the people by Moses there is an outburst of horror and remorse. Then by a sudden reversal of feeling they determine to attempt an entrance into the land from which they have been excluded by divine decree. "And they rose up early in the morning, and gat them up into the top of the mountain, saying, Lo, we be here, and will go up unto the place which the Lord hath promised: for we have sinned."

This rash presumption is as serious an exhibition of unbelief as had been their former fear and their mad determination to return to Egypt. "And Moses said, Wherefore now do ye transgress the commandment of the Lord? but it shall not prosper. Go not up, for the Lord is not among you; that ye be not smitten before your enemies. For the Amalekites and the Canaanites are there before you, and ye shall fall by the sword: because ye are turned away from the Lord, therefore the Lord will not be with you."

In spite of this explicit warning, the people defied Moses and openly rebelled against God. They had not repented. True repentance is shown not only in regret that one has forfeited a great opportunity and has brought upon himself distress and irreparable loss, but by patient submission to the divine will. Pardon restores one to a right relation with God, but it does not avert the inevitable consequences of an evil course. Faith accepts what God may decree and trusts in His grace to suffer and to endure and to find in fellowship with Him strength and guidance and peace. "But they presumed to go up onto the hill top: nevertheless the ark of the covenant of the Lord, and Moses, departed not out of the camp. Then the Amalekites came down and the Canaanites which dwelt in the hill, and smote them, and discomfited them, even unto Hormah."

This tragic repulse from the borders of Canaan was a turning point in the history of redemption. No wonder that it was regarded through the following centuries as a warning against unbelief. Again and again when men have been brought to the threshold of some great adventure they have lacked faith in God, have failed to press forward and consequently have carried through their remaining days the bitter memory of what might have been.

Canaan may represent to us a life of true fellowship with Christ. He calls us to enter on such an experience. He tells us what the spies reported, both the richness of the land and the enemies which are to be overcome. He assures us that to follow Him is to have life which is life indeed, but He warns us to count the cost. There will be battles and burdens and hardships, but an eternal recompense for those who go forward with trust in Him.

Canaan also can represent the heavenly "rest" and blessedness which are promised to the followers of Christ. It was natural for the psalmist and the apostle to use this painful historic episode as a warning against unbelief: "Wherefore (as the Holy Ghost saith, Today if ye will hear his voice, harden not your hearts, as in the provocation, in the day of temptation in the wilderness: when your fathers tempted me, proved me, and saw my works forty years. Wherefore I was grieved with that generation, and said, They do alway err in their hearts: and they have not known my ways. So I sware in my wrath. They shall not enter into my rest.) Take heed, brethren, lest there be in any of you an evil heart of unbelief, in departing from the living God" (Heb. 3:7-12). "Let us therefore fear, lest, a promise being left us of entering into his rest, any of you should seem to come short of it. For unto us was the gospel preached, as well as unto them: but the word preached did not profit them, not being mixed with faith in them that heard it. . . . Let us labour therefore to enter into that rest" (Heb. 4:1, 2, 11).

## LAWS AND SANCTIONS [Ch. 15]

The place in the story where these ordinances are recorded, and the time and place where they were to be observed, give an inspiring indication of the love and grace of God. The people had failed. In unbelief they had turned back from the border of Canaan to die in the desert. This sentence of death had been pronounced upon all those twenty years old and upward who had come out of Egypt. The explicit word of the Lord was this: "Doubtless ye shall not come unto the land concerning which I sware to make you dwell therein." Now follow these laws which were to be kept, according to the divine command: "When ye come into the land of your habitations which I give you." This sudden contrast is an eloquent expression of the pardoning mercy of God, and of His unchanging purpose. The nation was not to be blotted out; a new generation was to rise. The promises of God to Israel were not to fail. The people were to be brought into the land of Canaan. There they were to show their gratitude and faith by a careful observance of the sacred laws and ordinances given to them in the wilderness. Of these the ones here specified related to sacrifices and offerings. They are described more definitely in the opening chapters of Leviticus. The "burnt offering" signified dedication; the "sin offering," expiation; the "peace offering," gratitude and communion. Here, however, unique emphasis is laid upon the *"meat offering,"* more correctly called the "meal" offering. It consisted of flour and grain; with it were associated gifts of oil and wine. It expressed the consecration to God of the fruits of human labor. Such "meal" offerings must accompany the other sacrifices. Thus, too, if one accepts Christ as his Sacrifice for sin, if he professes to yield himself in dedication to his divine Lord, one also must show the "good works" and generous deeds and holy conduct which are the evidences of a living faith (Ch. 15:1-21).

As to the sacrifices to be offered in atonement for sin, a clear distinction is made between *sins of omission, or ignorance,* and sins which were *presumptuous,* intentional and in defiance of God. Ignorance of the law was not an excuse for a breach of the law. Sins of omission and sins of ignorance were none the less sins. The offenders must bring a sin offering; the priest could "make an atonement" for him and forgiveness could be secured. For one who sinned presumptuously, "with a high hand," as though lifting up his hand in defiance of God, no atonement was possible, no sacrifices could be offered; he must be "cut off from among his people" (Ch. 15:22-31).

The Gospel has a message infinitely more hopeful. Even the most wilful and presumptuous sin can be forgiven in view of the atoning work of Christ. How fatal, then, must be the refusal to accept the redemption one has secured by Christ's own precious

blood! "He that despised Moses' law died without
mercy under two or three witnesses; of how much
sorer punishment, suppose ye, shall he be thought
worthy, who hath trodden under foot the Son of
God, and hath counted the blood of the covenant,
wherewith he was sanctified, an unholy thing, and
hath done despite unto the Spirit of grace?" Let us
remember with humble gratitude that our Great
High Priest "is able also to save them to the uttermost that come unto God by him, seeing he ever
liveth to make intercession for them" (Heb. 10:28,
29; 7:25).

*The punishment* of the *Sabbath-breaker* is recorded here as an illustration of the severe penalty
attached by the law of Moses to wilful and presumptuous sin. The offender could not possibly claim ignorance of the statute to which already the death
penalty had been added (Ex. 31:15). His sin was in
open defiance of God. His execution was delayed,
not because of any uncertainty as to his guilt, or its
necessary punishment, but because Moses waited to
learn the manner of the penalty to be imposed. The
verdict was, "All the congregation shall stone him
with stones."

Let us not hastily condemn this cruel punishment of an apparently trifling fault; we need to
remember the recent and solemn warnings of the sacred law. Nor are we lightly to dismiss the obligation
of Sabbath observance as an antiquated fragment of
a Jewish ritual. Our Saviour, who claimed to be
"Lord of the Sabbath," taught by precept and example that the day, made the more sacred as a memorial

of His resurrection, is to be observed as a season of worship and of rest, broken only by deeds of necessity and mercy (Mark 2:23 to 3:5).

The last of these laws (Ch. 15:37-41) required the Israelites to wear, on the corners of their garments, *tassels* ("fringes") tied by a cord of blue. These were intended to be reminders of the commandments of the Lord, who had "brought them out of the land of Egypt." Great sanctity was attached to these tassels. They were "enlarged" by the Pharisees in the time of Christ that the wearer might "be seen of men" and gain a reputation for holiness. The very institution which was designed to turn the thoughts toward God was used to minister to the pride and vanity of men. Thus it often happens that the spirit of a religious custom is completely lost, while the outward form is retained.

Another purpose was served by these tassels. They distinguished the Jewish people from other races. This was quite proper, and it may be added that in the simplest matter of daily life and conduct there always should be something about the followers of Christ to intimate that they are in reality the people of God.

## THE REBELLION OF KORAH [Ch. 16]

After the Israelites had been repelled from the borders of Canaan in defeat and disgrace, some thirty-seven years were passed in wandering and sojourning in the wilderness. It is remarkable that the history is practically silent as to the events of this long pe-

riod. One crisis in the national life, however, is
recorded. It is deeply significant and its messages
are relevant to present-day problems. This event
was the rebellion against the power and leadership
of Moses and Aaron. The rebellion was led by
Korah, a member of the tribe of Levi. He associated
with himself two hundred and fifty princes who
represented different tribes, and are described as "fa-
mous in the congregation, men of renown." He was
further aided by Dathan and Abiram, members of
the tribe of Reuben. Korah, as a Levite, was jealous
of the privileges granted to Aaron as the high priest.
He reasons that "all the congregation were holy,
every one of them," and all equally were the servants
of the Lord. Therefore, Aaron and his sons had no
right to assume positions from which their fellow
Levites were excluded. The charge was expressed
in these words, "Ye take too much upon you."

The revolt of Dathan and Abiram was due to
their jealousy of Moses. They were descended from
Reuben, the eldest son of Jacob. Moses belonged to
the tribe of Levi and thus was descended from a
younger son. They objected to the fact that Moses
had been placed in a position superior to themselves.

In dealing with this twofold conspiracy, Moses
first of all turns to Korah and his confederate princes.
He challenges them to assume the duties of priesthood to which Aaron and his sons had been appointed. He commands them to appear upon the
morrow with censers in which fire is to be placed and
in which incense is to be burned. He declares that
God will show whether Aaron or his enemies have

been divinely chosen. The choice of the Lord will indicate who are "holy"; and he turns against the traitors the very words which Korah had used, "Ye take too much upon you, ye sons of Levi." Having given this challenge, Moses shows the real character of the rebellion. He reveals the essential nature of all jealousy and envy. It is in reality rebellion against God. Moses reminds Korah that the sons of Levi have been divinely appointed to perform certain sacred and honorable tasks. They have been set aside "to do the service of the tabernacle of the Lord, and to stand before the congregation to minister unto them." This divine appointment should have been gratefully accepted. They should not have been envious of Aaron and his sons who had been assigned specific tasks: "Seek ye the priesthood also? For which cause both thou and all thy company are gathered together against the Lord: and what is Aaron, that ye murmur against him?"

This is the essence of jealousy. It is rebellion against the providence of God. He has given to each one of us definite tasks to perform and differing talents to be employed. Why should we seek to fill the places assigned to others? Why should we be envious of the abilities which they possess? It is for us gratefully to accept the positions divinely apportioned and to believe that it is honor enough faithfully to accomplish our own allotted work; and, further, we should be assured that, for the accomplishment of the work which He assigns, God will give us abilities and grace and strength for its achievement.

Moses next turns to deal with Dathan and

Abiram. As the commander of the people, he sum-
mons them to his presence. They reply with inso-
lence and defiance, "We will not come up." They
accuse Moses of cruelty, dishonesty and selfish ambition. They make the absurd statement that he has
brought them out of Egypt, "a land that floweth with
milk and honey"; he wishes to destroy them in the
wilderness or at least to make himself their king; he
has not fulfilled his promise; he has not brought
them into a land of plenty; he has not given them
an inheritance of fields and vineyards. He is attempting to blind them or make them slaves. They repeat
their defiance, "We will not come up." Moses in-
dignantly denies their false charge. He insists that
he has never robbed or injured any of the people.

Moses was innocent of the charge. Yet there is
something quite modern in their description of a
tyrant: he makes false promises; he seeks personal
advantage and power. Moses, however, was the just
and unselfish representative of God the King. Korah
may represent disloyalty to the Church; Dathan and
Abiram are types of rebellion against the state.

On the morrow Korah and his followers accept
the challenge. They appear with their censers and
upon them they place the fire, and they take their
stand at the door of the tabernacle. Throngs of Israelites crowd about them. These men, contrary to
the divine provision, are about to undertake the most
sacred act of the prescribed ritual. They are to offer
incense, which was the peculiar prerogative of the
priests. Moses and Aaron are bidden to withdraw
from the congregation, as the Lord is about to de-

stroy His rebellious people; but Moses and Aaron plead for their preservation. The people are not destroyed, only the leaders of the rebellion: "there came out a fire from the Lord and consumed the two hundred and fifty men that offered incense."

Moses then approaches the tents of the defiant rebels, Dathan and Abiram. He urges the people to withdraw to a distance. He insists that dire judgment is to be visited upon these enemies of order. He declares that if these men "die the common death of all men, or if they be visited after the visitation of all men," then it can be concluded that Moses is not the divinely appointed leader of Israel.

On the other hand, "if the Lord make a new thing, and the earth open her mouth, and swallow them up, with all that appertain unto them, and they go down living into the pit, then ye shall understand that these men have provoked the Lord. And it came to pass, as he had made an end of speaking all these words, that the ground clave asunder that was under them: and the earth opened her mouth and swallowed them up, and their houses . . . and all that appertained to them went down alive into the pit, and the earth closed upon them: and they perished from among the congregation. And all Israel that were round about them fled at the cry of them: for they said, Lest the earth swallow us up also."

This terrifying and tragic penalty which fell upon Korah, Dathan, and Abiram proclaims obvious messages which are a warning to the people of God of all the ages.

First of all, it indicates what has been truly declared, namely, that jealousy is suicide. It brings bitterness and pain and distress into one's own heart, and takes the joy and gladness out of life. It is among the most universal of passions, and its issue is as pitiful as it is certain.

A lesson which is quite as pertinent to the present day concerns the relation which Christians, as the people of God, should sustain toward the church and the state, represented in this story by Aaron and Moses. Both church and state are of divine origin. They are, however, to be kept distinct and separate. The church is to exercise no control over the state, and the state should endeavor in no wise to influence the church. The followers of Christ must be devoted and loyal to both these divine institutions.

Loyalty to the church is possible only when one realizes the truth on which Korah based his false claim. All the people of God are equals in His sight; but it is not true that the same duties are assigned to all or that all should claim identical positions and tasks. In the days of shadow and symbol, Korah and the Levites should have been content with the tasks assigned and should not have sought the office of the priesthood to which others had been appointed. They should have been content with their equality as those to whom honorable functions in the public worship of God had been given. They should have claimed neither equality with Aaron nor superiority to their brothers.

As followers of Christ we should believe in the universal priesthood of believers. All are on a spir-

itual equality because all are equally subject to our
great High Priest. In His service, different functions
are to be performed by the various members of this
royal priesthood. In His church the offices which are
held are simply those of ministers or servants. They
indicate no superior cast. Each one should be content with the place assigned, and should entertain
no jealousy of those who are called to a differing
ministry. Real dependence on the guidance of their
great High Priest will banish from the hearts of worshipers all envy and bitterness and pride and selfish
ambition and ill will.

The followers of Christ must be loyal not only
to the church but also to the state. They must be
willing to accept whatever burdens the state may im-
pose and to make any necessary sacrifice it may require. Dathan and Abiram should not have defied
the authority of Moses on the specious plea that they
were his equals since they belonged to "the congregation of the Lord." So, today, equality before the
law is not an excuse for defying the officers of the
law. Those who, with the cry of "equality," plot to
overthrow a legally established government are usually guilty of the faults which Dathan and Abiram
attributed to Moses, namely, false promises, cruelty,
and a selfish assumption of tyrannical power. It is
the privilege of Christians to aid in the establishment
of just laws, and to regard rulers who obey these
laws as "the ministers of God for good" (Rom.
13:1-7).

The two hundred and fifty censers which had
been used by Korah and his companions in their sac-

rilegious act were preserved as a memorial of this mournful episode in the life of Israel. These censers were designated by the historian as "holy." This was because they had been presented in worship before the door of the tabernacle, but at the cost of the lives of their owners. Because of this relation to the dead, Aaron, the great high priest against whom Korah had rebelled, was not allowed to be defiled by touching these censers. His son, Eleazar, was assigned the sad task of their collection and removal. They were rolled into plates and placed on the sides of the brazen altar, not only further to protect the wooden frame of the altar, but to bear continual witness to the law that incense could be offered only by a priest and that each one of God's people should be content with the place and task divinely assigned. These plates of brass were to be a warning against envy and jealousy and against the presumption of thrusting one's self into a position to which he has not been called.

However, the people of Israel were not willing to be warned. They had seen the appalling punishment which had come to Korah, Dathan, and Abiram for rebelling against their divinely appointed leaders; but on the very next day they renew the attack on Moses and Aaron, accusing them of being responsible for the death of the rebels, saying, "Ye have killed the people of the Lord."

As will be remembered, the very life of the people had been spared on the day before only because of the intercession of Moses and Aaron. To hold them responsible for the penalty which had been imposed on the leaders of the insurrection was as definite a defiance of God as the rebellion of Korah had been. As might have been expected, there was an overwhelming manifestation of the divine presence shining forth from the cloud of glory and a declaration that the penalty of death was about to be imposed upon the insolent multitude.

Again Moses and Aaron offer their plea that the people should not be consumed. At the bidding of Moses, Aaron takes his censer. He places in it coals from off the sacred altar and on it he places incense, and he rushes toward the multitude in a dramatic act of intercession. "And Aaron took as Moses commanded, and ran into the midst of the congregation; and behold, the plague was begun among the people: and he put on incense, and made an atonement for the people. And he stood between the dead and the living; and the plague was stayed." Evidently the people had been smitten by a deadly pestilence and the very existence of a nation was again in peril. Even when the plague had been arrested more than fourteen thousand had forfeited their lives.

That is a memorable picture, as Aaron the high priest is seen standing "between the dead and the living" and making intercession which is effectual and by which further destruction is averted. This picture has been taken as a symbol of our Great High Priest and Intercessor. He not only stood in danger of death as the Mediator for His people, but He endured for their sake the darkness and the agonies of death. Wherefore "he became the author of eternal salvation unto all them that obey him."

## THE BUDDING OF AARON'S ROD [Ch. 17]

The divine appointment of Aaron to the priest-hood was attested in many ways. His choice had been announced to Moses by the voice of God; he had been consecrated to the holy office by an impressive ritual; he had been anointed with the sacred oil and clothed with the resplendent garments of "glory and beauty." Because of their disregard for the laws of his ministry his two sons, Dathan and Abiram, had been smitten with instant death. Korah and his con-federates, who in jealousy had rebelled against Aaron, were destroyed by fire. His priestly intercession and offering of incense had preserved the life of the na-tion. The final witness to his unique position was the miraculous budding of his rod.

As divinely commanded, Moses requested each of the princes who represented one of the tribes of Israel to bring a rod on which the name of the prince was written. On the rod of the tribe of Levi the name of Aaron was inscribed. As the rods were to be twelve in number, it would seem that Ephraim and Manasseh were to be reckoned here as the one "tribe of Joseph" (Deut. 27:12). Levi, as the priestly tribe, exempt from military service, was commonly omitted from the enumeration. Here, however, as the tribe to which the priesthood belonged, Levi was specifically mentioned and on its rod was written the name of Aaron the high priest.

These twelve rods were then laid up in the tab-ernacle before the Lord who promised that He would signify by a divine act which was His choice to be the priestly tribe. The purpose was to silence from henceforth all jealous "murmurings" against Aaron and his sons as the appointed priests of God. "And it came to pass, that on the morrow Moses went into the tabernacle of witness; and, behold, the rod of Aaron for the house of Levi was budded, and brought forth buds, and bloomed blossoms, and yielded almonds."

"And Moses brought out all the rods from before the Lord unto all the children of Israel: and they looked, and took every man his rod.

"And the Lord said unto Moses, Bring Aaron's rod again before the testimony, to be kept for a token against the rebels; and thou shalt take away their murmurings from me, that they die not."

Therefore, the rod which had budded became a continual memorial and seal of the divinely appointed and attested priesthood of Aaron.

Such marvelous attestations and sanctions gave a holy dignity and honor to the office of Aaron, which assumed a new glory when it became a symbol and a type of the redeeming work of Christ. The inspiring theme of the Epistle to the Hebrews is the Highpriesthood of Christ. It can be understood only by continual reference to the history of Aaron. His sacrifice, his intercession, his mediation, were all shadows of the realities which were embodied in Christ; and the first point of the inspired comparison was that which was pictured by the budding of Aaron's rod. This miracle was a token of his divine appointment, so it was a symbol of the divine commission of our Lord. Thus, in referring to the priesthood of Christ, the Apostle declares: "No man taketh this honor unto himself, but he that is called of God as was Aaron. So also Christ glorified not himself to be made an high priest but he that said unto him, Thou art my Son, today have I begotten thee" (Heb. 5:4, 5).

No other agent, or representative, or ritual has been divinely appointed or is needed. Through Christ we have immediate and unrestricted access to God; "for there is one God and one mediator between God and men, the man Jesus Christ" (I Tim. 2:5).

Having therefore, brethren, boldness to enter into the holiest by the blood of Jesus, by a new and living way, which he hath consecrated for us, through the veil, that is to say his flesh; and having an high priest over the house of God; let us draw near with a true heart in full assurance of faith, having our hearts sprinkled from an evil conscience, and our bodies washed with pure water.

Let us hold fast the profession of our faith without wavering; (for he is faithful that promised;) and let us consider one another to provoke unto love and to good works: not forsaking the assembling of ourselves together, as the manner of some is; but exhorting one another; and so much the more, as ye see the day approaching (Heb. 10:19-25).

## Duties and Privileges of Priests and Levites
### [Ch. 18]

The budding of Aaron's rod not only confirmed his divine appointment to the priesthood, it also attested the choice of the tribe of Levi as the sole priestly tribe. On the rod had been inscribed the name of Aaron, but it also was the rod which had been selected to represent the tribe of Levi. Its miraculous blossoms vindicated the claims of Aaron and his sons to the priesthood and designated the remaining members of the tribe to be their helpers in the sacred ministry of the tabernacle. Naturally the chapter which follows details the duties and privileges of these priests and Levites.

Furthermore, it answers the solemn question with which the story had closed: "And the children of Israel spake unto Moses, saying, Behold, we die, we perish, we all perish. Whosoever cometh any thing near unto the tabernacle of the Lord shall die: shall we be consumed with dying?" (Ch. 17:13).

The dreadful punishment of Korah and his confederates and of those who had sympathized with them had caused the people to react from their rash presumption and they were in a state of abject terror. If those who attempted to assume the duties of priests and Levites had been visited by death, was it safe for anyone to approach "the tabernacle of the Lord"? Would they not "be consumed with dying"?

The reply is contained in the following chapter. It shows that God had appointed ministers of His sanctuary. If the people would regard and support these representatives, it would be possible to approach God in worship and to enjoy the peace of His pardoning grace and the privilege of fellowship with Him.

A familiar parallel commonly is found in religious experience. Every act of divine judgment, every manifestation of God's presence, awakens fear in the minds of men. They feel a sense of dread. Fellowship with a holy God seems impossible for those who are conscious of sin. Then comes the good news of the Gospel. God has provided a Great High Priest. If we accept Him, serve Him, and trust in His atoning work, we can "come boldly unto the throne of grace, that we may obtain mercy, and find grace to help in time of need" (Heb. 4:16).

The *duty* assigned to Aaron and his sons was to "bear the iniquity of the sanctuary" and "the iniquity of the priesthood" (v. 1). That is, they were to be responsible for any irregularity in divine worship or any intrusion into their sacred office such as that attempted by Korah. If they rightly fulfilled their assigned tasks then there would "be no wrath any more upon the children of Israel" (v. 5).

These *tasks* of the priesthood had been fully set forth in the Book of Leviticus. They included "the charge of the sanctuary and the charge of the altar" (v. 5). Only the priests could offer sacrifices; only they could trim the lamps and present the shew-bread and burn incense in the Holy Place; only the High Priest could pass "within the veil" (v. 7) and make intercession for the people, in the Holy of Holies, before the ark of the covenant. Thus the duties of the priests included all the ceremonies which were to be performed at "the altar" (of burnt offerings) and in the sanctuary "within the veil" (v. 7), and all those observed between these two points, such as the services of the Holy Place. All these prescribed tasks were to be regarded as privileges. They belonged to the "priest's office," which was "a service of gift." It was not a matter of choice or merely an inheritance; it was not a burden; it was a bestowal granted by the grace of God; it was so sacred that "a stranger" (anyone not thus divinely appointed) who should come nigh to assume its duties should be "put to death." The tasks assigned the Levites were those of assistants to the priests. They were "a gift for the Lord to do the service of the tabernacle" (v. 6), but they could not "come nigh the vessels of the sanctuary," nor could they minister at the altar. Such a sacrilege would be punished by the death of the offender and the death of the priest by whom it was permitted.

The statement that the priesthood was to be regarded as a divine "gift" to ancient Israel reminds one of the New Testament view of the Christian ministry. However much those thus serving the church may differ in their tasks and their talents, all are to be considered as gifts from the ascended Christ. "He gave some [to be] apostles; and some, prophets; and some, evangelists; and some, pastors and teachers; for the perfecting of the saints, for the work of the ministry, for the edifying of the body of Christ" (Eph. 4:11, 12).

To Aaron and his sons (vs. 8-20) were assigned the "heave offerings," consisting of the "meal offerings," and the "guilt offerings" which the worshipers brought to the tabernacle. These, when first presented to the Lord, were then to be eaten in the sacred precincts, by the priests alone (v. 10).

The "wave offerings," which were portions of

the "peace offerings," could be eaten by the priests and by the members of their families, in their homes, provided that those who partook were ceremonially clean. The perquisites of the priests also included the first-fruits of the land, and all things which had been devoted to the Lord by vows. Furthermore, the first-born of man and of beast belonged to Aaron and his sons; but first-born children were to be redeemed by the payment of "five shekels"; and of unclean animals, the first-born could be redeemed, as they likewise could not be offered as sacrifices (vs. 15-19).

In view of such provision for their support, no land was to be allotted to the priests. They were relieved from earning their livelihood by agriculture. The Lord was to be their "part" and their "inheritance." He had assigned to them sacred duties, He had directed that their wants should be supplied by the offerings of the worshipers, and as He the "Lord of all" was their inheritance, they were possessors of all things.

This ordinance for the support of the priests is quite in accordance with the New Testament provisions. Those who preach the Gospel and devote their lives to the service of the church should be supported liberally by the gifts of the people whom they serve. As Paul wrote to the Corinthians: "Do ye not know that they which minister about holy things live of the things of the temple? and they which wait at the altar are partakers with the altar? Even so hath the Lord ordained that they which preach the gospel should live of the gospel" (I Cor. 9:13, 14).

What *portion* of one's income should be devoted

to such support of religion? This is intimated in the regulation made for the sustenance of the Levites (vs. 20-32). A tenth part of all increase from fruits and flocks was to be given them yearly by every one of the children of Israel. According to earlier laws, such tithes had been claimed by the Lord (Lev. 27:30, 32) but now all these tithes were specifically assigned to the Levites in recognition of their services. Like the priests they had homes and cities, and certain pasture lands near these cities, but no fields of their own to be cultivated. They were to live, not by manual labor, but wholly on the tithes required to be given them by the people whom they represented and served in the sacred offices of the tabernacle.

However, from the tithes which they received, the Levites, in turn, were to give a tenth part for the further support of the priests. Such tithes were regarded as an offering to the Lord, and while given to the Levites by the people, they were to be considered to be as truly their own gifts as though each one had presented the produce of his own "threshing-floor" and "winepress."

Thus all of the Israelites were tithed to support the Levites and the Levites in turn were tithed to support the priests.

Such a system has been regarded as a guide to the followers of Christ. It has been concluded that the law of the Israelites should bind all Christians to tithe their incomes for the support of the church. Probably one tenth is a fair proportion to be given as an average; but for many Christians this might involve undue hardship on dependents, and for others it may be far too small a proportion of their increasing wealth. According to New Testament standards, each one should give "as the Lord has prospered him." Such giving should be systematic, and thoughtful, and conscientious. For the Christian Church a rigid law of tithing has given place to the principle of stewardship. Each one should regard his income and all his possessions as a sacred trust. For its use he is responsible to his Lord, to whom he must render an account. Certain sums must be set aside for specifically religious purposes. These may be actual or relative "tithes." They must be "brought into the storehouse" of the Lord if one is to expect a "blessing" to be "poured out" from "the windows of heaven" (Mal. 3:10).

## THE WATER OF PURIFICATION [Ch. 19]

To understand the meaning of "the water of purification" one needs to remember the relation between sin and death set forth in the Scripture; as, for example, in the following passages: "The wages of sin is death" (Rom. 6:23); "The sting of death is sin" (I Cor. 15:56); "By one man sin entered into the world, and death by sin" (Rom. 5:12; and Gen. 2:17).

Therefore, in a system of symbols representing the relation of men to God it was natural that contact with the dead made one ceremonially "unclean" and unfit to approach the Tabernacle. Such contact was not sinful. It involved no moral fault. Indeed, it might have been demanded by duty or affection;

but it typified the effect of sin which separates one from his fellow worshipers and interrupts his communion with God.

For the removal of such ceremonial uncleanness, a unique and elaborate ritual was prescribed. A "red heifer" was chosen of which the color and freedom from blemish made it a symbol of vigorous life. It was killed "outside the camp" as an offering for sin. Eleazar, the son of Aaron, presided at the ceremony, as participation in the ordinance might have involved ceremonial uncleanness and thus have interrupted the high priest in his duties. The blood of the sacrifice was sprinkled seven times toward the Tabernacle, instead of being sprinkled on the altar as was usual with the blood of offerings; but, likewise, this symbolized intercession, and atonement by the life which had been offered. The entire heifer then was burned, and, to enrich the significance of the ritual, cedar wood and hyssop and threads of scarlet were cast into the fire. Cedar was regarded as having healing qualities and was a fragrant symbol of incorruption; hyssop was associated with purification; and scarlet was an emblem of sin (Is. 1:18), but also of blood which is "the life," and was offered for the remission of sin.

When the sacrifice and these accompaniments had been consumed with fire, the ashes which remained were "laid up without the camp in a clean place," and kept for the specific use of ceremonial purification. When needed, this was done by dissolving a portion of the ashes in a vessel of pure water, and by sprinkling on the unclean person or object this "water of separation." More exactly, it was water which ended the separation caused by contact with the dead.

All persons who had taken part in the ceremony or who touched the water must be bathed and regarded as unclean until the evening of the day; but anyone who had been defiled by contact with the dead, if sprinkled on the third day and again on the seventh day, was declared to be ceremonially clean, and was restored to the privileges of fellowship and of worship.

The New Testament interpretation of this ancient ceremony was very definite and practical: "If the blood of bulls and of goats, and the ashes of an heifer sprinkling the unclean, sanctifieth to the purifying of the flesh: how much more shall the blood of Christ, who through the eternal Spirit offered himself without spot to God, purge your conscience from dead works to serve the living God?" (Heb. 9:13, 14).

This is to say, if sprinkling this water of purification could make clean a physical body which had been tainted by contact with the dead, much more could "the blood of Christ" cleanse the conscience which had been stained by "dead works" of sin and spiritual uncleanness.

The application to Christian experience becomes the more impressive when one notes that this peculiar ceremonial of the water of purification was recorded, not in the Book of Leviticus, which is a manual for worship and a handbook of sacrifices and offerings, but here in Numbers, which is a book of history relating to the wilderness experiences of the children of Israel. By it the followers of Christ who are journeying through this world towards the heavenly Canaan are warned to avoid the contacts with evil by which one may be separated from fellow worshipers and deprived of communion with God. It encourages everyone whose conscience has been stained by such contacts to seek that cleansing which the blood of Christ affords. This is possible by applying to the soul the precious truth concerning the atoning work of our Lord, who "by his own blood" has obtained "eternal redemption for us" (Heb. 9:12).

# III

## *ON THE BORDERS OF CANAAN*
### NUMBERS 20:1 to 36:13

### THE SIN OF MOSES AND AARON [Ch. 20:1-13]

THE twentieth chapter of Numbers is one of the most distressing pages in the history of Israel. As it opens, it records the death of Miriam; it closes with an account of the death of Aaron, and includes the story of the supreme failure in the life of Moses. Both brothers were included in the fault, but the elder brother, Aaron, seems to have been a silent but none the less guilty actor in the scene. He long had held the supreme place in the nation as the leader of religious worship. He was an eloquent and gifted man but lacked strength of character and usually reflected the mood of those about him. At the request of the people he led them in the worship of the golden calf. He accompanied Miriam in her jealous and cruel attack on Moses.

The younger brother, Moses, stands out in unsurpassed majesty among the heroes of his race. Yet the greatest of men may suffer defeat and disgrace and this too at the very point where their chief strength is supposed to lie. So it was with Moses. His meekness and consecration were regarded as matchless; yet he was overcome by anger and was disobedient to God.

86

The sad story of his fall never should be read
without first reminding one's self of the grandeur of
his character and the glory of his achievements. Otherwise, one may lose the inspiration of his noble life
and the solemn warning of his failure and defeat.

Moses was great as a soldier and statesman; he
delivered his people from bondage and disciplined
a great army, leading them through a wilderness to
the border of the promised land. He was a poet
whose songs still instruct and cheer the people of
God. He was a lawgiver whose code underlies the
jurisprudence of all civilized nations. As a historian
his records are priceless. As an author his short
stories are unsurpassed. Most important of all, he
was known as "the man of God." So truly was he a
type of Christ that he could predict "a prophet shall
the Lord God raise up unto you of your brethren
like unto me," and the apostle could say of Christ
that he "was faithful to him that appointed him as
also Moses was faithful in all his house."

What, then, was the offense which caused him to
forfeit the supreme hope of his life and to be excluded from the land of promise? The answer is not
altogether obvious or clear. At least, it is certain that
when exasperated by the faithless multitude he gave
way to anger, which was expressed in word and in
action; but the fault was more serious than at first
appears. It was recorded as "unbelief" (v. 12), and
rebellion (Ch. 27:14), and a failure to "sanctify God."
It can be estimated and understood only as one remembers the peculiar position and privilege of Moses
as the representative, the mouthpiece and agent of

the Lord. This high calling and commission Moses
was forgetting and abandoning when he allowed himself to become enraged by the hostility and re-
proaches of the people.

They were not wholly without excuse. Their
plight was pitiful in the extreme. When encamping
in the wilderness their supply of water had failed.
We can picture the scene—little children crying in
distress, cattle falling by the wayside, strong men and
women frenzied with thirst—"death in the desert."
However, the charge against Moses was cruel and un-
just. "And they gathered themselves together against
Moses and against Aaron. And the people chode
with Moses, and spake, saying, Would God that we
had died when our brethren died before the Lord!
And why have ye brought up the congregation of the
Lord into this wilderness, that we and our cattle
should die there? And wherefore have ye made us
to come up out of Egypt, to bring us in unto this evil
place? It is no place of seed, or of figs, or of vines, or
of pomegranates; neither is there any water to
drink." The falseness of this mad complaint is evident when one remembers that the people were in
the wilderness through no fault of Moses, but because of their own stubbornness and unbelief. They
were suffering a divine penalty for their lack of faith
and obedience. In their reference to the fruit of
Canaan there was a tinge of irony and an implied
charge that the promises of Moses had not been fulfilled.

The patient but deeply offended leader made
no reply. As often before, in times of great trial and

crisis, he turned in silence to the place of worship and prayer, and fell prostrate before the Lord. "Moses and Aaron went from the presence of the assembly unto the door of the tabernacle of the congregation, and they fell upon their faces: and the glory of the Lord appeared unto them."

Moses there was given a new vision of God, and at the same time he received a specific command and a divine promise. "And the Lord spake unto Moses, saying, Take the rod, and gather thou the assembly together, thou, and Aaron thy brother, and speak ye unto the rock before their eyes; and it shall give forth his water, and thou shalt bring forth to them water out of the rock: so thou shalt give the congregation and their beasts drink."

It was an hour of incomparable possibilities. He could have brought to the people a new and impressive message of the goodness and grace of God, but at the sight of the multitude and remembering the treachery and disloyalty of the Israelites he was overwhelmed by a storm of anger, and he seemed to forget the message of the Lord and to recall only the words of the disloyal and hostile tribes. As he and Aaron met the congregation, he cried out with bitter rebuke, "Hear now, ye rebels; must we fetch you water out of this rock? And Moses lifted up his hand, and with his rod he smote the rock twice: and the water came out abundantly, and the congregation drank and their beasts also." Moses had much reason for anger. Again and again he had interceded for the faithless people. He had been their deliverer, their savior, their unselfish guide. Now again they had turned from him in faithless revolt and were ready to destroy him in their hatred and distrust. They had tried him beyond his power to endure. The fault of his behavior was in large measure theirs. As the Psalmist declared: "They angered him also at the waters of strife, so that it went ill with Moses for their sakes: because they provoked his spirit, so that he spake unadvisedly with his lips."

Nevertheless, his offense was great. In his anger he calls the people "rebels." This they were. Yet at the very time Moses himself was in rebellion against God. Forgetting his high calling as a representative of the Lord and arrogating to himself honor which belonged to God alone, he cries, "Must we fetch you water out of this rock?" It is true that the pronoun "we" is not in the original Hebrew, and therefore is not to be emphasized too far; yet the question surely contains no suggestion of the goodness and power of God. Moses was claiming ability to work a miracle, or at least was willing to have it regarded as his own work.

In addition to this disloyal question there was the rebellious act. He had been told to speak to the rock, but instead of this "he smote the rock twice." Undoubtedly he was acting in fierce anger; yet anger is always a symptom of deeper seated disease. There was something of wounded pride as he called the people "rebels." There was presumption in the offer to work a miracle. There was self-will and disobedience in his smiting the rock.

Yet "the water came out abundantly." In spite of the unfaithfulness of His servant, God was true to

His promise. He showed himself gracious and He preserved the nation to which He had assured an entrance into Canaan. On the other hand, God was just. He could not overlook the grievous fault which seemed to indicate that in spite of all his great services Moses was unfitted for the difficult task of conquering the land of promise. He pronounced upon Moses and Aaron the solemn sentence, "Because ye believed me not, to sanctify me in the eyes of the children of Israel, therefore ye shall not bring this congregation into the land which I have given them."

The penalty may seem to have been too severe, yet the seriousness of the offense must be kept in mind. The severity of the punishment emphasizes the warning which should come to all the people of God. "Let him who thinketh he standeth take heed lest he fall." Moses believed himself to be meek, indeed, to be "the meekest of men." He did not know himself. He seems to have forgotten the experience of forty years before. His uncontrolled anger and his rash attack on the Egyptian had resulted in forty years of exile from Egypt, and now, after a long period of discipline, the old passionate, presumptuous nature is again revealed and Moses loses the prize for which he had been striving all his life. How unexpectedly some old weakness may reappear and overcome the truest servant of God! Surely we need to "watch and pray."

The sequel of this painful story is found in the last chapter of Deuteronomy, where we read of the death of Moses, alone on the mountain, and of his burial in an unknown grave; but the intervening history has shown the majesty of his heroic character. Even when under the divine sentence for his fault, and when certain to suffer the ultimate penalty for his failure, the undaunted leader, forgiven and in fellowship with God, resumes his task, leads and delivers his people and secures for them deliverance and victory until they are encamped on the plains of Moab ready to cross the Jordan into the land of promise. There he is given a vision. From a high mountain top he is permitted to view the land which the Lord had given to Abraham and Isaac and Jacob and their seed. There in the mountain solitude he died. There he was buried by angels. His life had not been a failure. Its main course had been a glorious triumph in fellowship with the Lord whom he served. The inspired epitaph reads as follows: "There arose not a prophet since in Israel like unto Moses, whom the Lord knew face to face."

Nor is this scene on Mount Pisgah the last in the inspired story. Centuries pass and "in the fullness of the time" the predicted Prophet appeared, the One who was greater than Moses, even as the anti-type surpasses the type. On a memorable occasion the Saviour stood on a holy mountain. It was located in the land of Canaan. Transfigured in divine glory, there appeared with Him Moses and Elijah, speaking of His death and His resurrection. Moses had entered the land by a celestial pathway. He had rejoiced in the experience of a "better country, that is a heavenly." He had become, too, a symbol of all the people of God who strive and serve, who fall and suffer and are forgiven, and who dwell at the last with the King in the true "land of promise."

The mention of Christ leads us to conclude the story of the riven rock with the message of the Apostle, who declared that the "rock was Christ," by which, of course, he meant that it was a type of Christ. He was once smitten for us and He has become the source of life-giving streams.

Moses in his anger impaired the type when he smote the rock a second time unbidden. He had been told to speak to the rock. Years before he had been directed to smite the rock with his rod. This action was not to be repeated. Christ was smitten for us, but this was once and for all. There can be no repetition of the Saviour's death. "But now once in the end of the world hath he appeared to put away sin by the sacrifice of himself. . . . So Christ was once offered to bear the sins of many." It is certain that all who trust and obey Him will experience the fulfilment of His promise, "Whosoever drinketh of the water that I shall give him shall never thirst; but the water that I shall give him shall be in him a well of water springing up into everlasting life."

## THE HOSTILITY OF EDOM [Ch. 20:14-21]

Now Israel begins the last stage of the journey toward the Land of Promise. The shortest route would have been due north; but that approach had failed before, and seems now to be blocked by the Canaanites (Ch. 21:1). Moses determines to go to the east, and then northward, and to enter the land by crossing the Jordan. This way led directly through the land of the Edomites; therefore Moses sends messengers to the king of Edom requesting permission to pass through his domain.

The request was reasonable and couched in courteous terms. Israel and Edom were kindred peoples; one was descended from Jacob ("Israel"), the other from Esau, and Jacob and Esau were twin brothers. Moses based his plea on this kinship, referring to their "fathers," and to "thy brother Israel." He appealed to sympathy by mentioning the long captivity by which Israel had been "vexed" in the land of Egypt. He intimated that they were under the direct guidance of God. Assurance was given that no harm would be done to fields or vineyards. When passage was refused, Moses offered to pay for any water taken from the wells, and again promised to follow closely the public road, "the king's high way."

In reply no civil or kindly word was sent to Moses, "and Edom came out against him with a strong hand." No attempt was made by Moses to force a passage. The simple record is this: "Thus Edom refused to give Israel passage through his border: wherefore Israel turned away from him."

Something is to be said in support of the contention that the king of Edom was acting with prudence and for the wise protection of his own people, whose country might have been desolated by the hordes of Israelites, even though the promise of Moses was sincere. Furthermore, it must be remembered that the Lord had warned Moses against attempting to conquer Edom or to trespass on the land (Deut. 2:4-6).

Yet the future references to the cruelty of Edom and to its predicted doom (Amos 1:11-12. Ob. 10-16), strengthen the impression that the course of the king was in harmony with the remembrance of how cruelly Jacob had treated Esau, and was dictated by hostility and jealousy and fear. The incident indicates the difficulties which continually beset Israel on its journey, and illustrates the obstacles and conflicts ever awaiting the people of God on their pilgrimage toward the "Better Land."

## THE DEATH OF AARON [Ch. 20:22-29]

Moving southward to pass around the territory of Edom, the Israelites reach Mount Hor, where Aaron died and was buried. It is a scene of deep pathos which the historian here sketches. Moses, the great Lawgiver, Aaron the first High Priest accompanied by his son Eleazar, climb together the lofty mountain. Both the great leaders had failed, both were under sentence of death and denied the privilege of entering the Land of Promise. Each was to die on a mountain top and to lie in a lonely grave. Yet the clouds of sunset must not obscure the glorious hours through which they had lived. These two were among the greatest heroes of history. They guided and preserved a people destined to exercise a supreme influence on the religious future of the world.

Nor must the superior greatness of Moses make

one unmindful of the part played by his elder brother Aaron. The latter had less moral stability, less powers of mind, but he was the first of that long line of priests who for ages maintained and controlled the only true religion of the race.

Theirs was a successive priesthood. It passed from father to son. On the mountain top, the robes of office were taken from Aaron and placed on Eleazar, who was thus ordained to assume all the duties and dignities which had belonged to his father. So it was through coming generations, priest took the place of priest, until at last a Great High Priest appeared whose ministry was not ended by death, but who continues to serve in the heavenly tabernacle, who has an "unchanging priesthood," who "ever liveth to make intercession" for His people.

### THE SERPENT OF BRASS [Ch. 21:1-9]

The Old Testament stories often are found to contain symbols of spiritual truth. The reader needs to exercise restraint lest his interpretations become mere flights of fancy, or lest an attempt be made to found a doctrine on a mere analogy. History must not be transformed into allegory. However, when our Lord employs the record of an event to illustrate His teaching, one is certain to discover a new depth of meaning, both in the narrative and in the truth which is thus impressed.

So it is with the story of the "serpent of brass." In it Christ found an arresting and illuminating type of His saving work. He gave utterance to the memorable words, "As Moses lifted up the serpent in the wilderness, even so must the Son of man be lifted up: that whosoever believeth in him should not perish, but have eternal life" (John 3:14, 15).

It is not difficult for us to reconstruct the ancient scene. The Israelites have resumed their journey toward Canaan. In response to their prayer God has given them victory over the hostile "king of Arad"; but as they have been denied a passage across the country of Edom, they are compelled to move southward before they can turn to the east and then to the north to find an entrance into the Land of Promise. They are in a desert, hot, sandy, arid, stony, infested by serpents and shut in by mountains. There is little food or water. What is most of all disheartening is the fact that for a time at least they have turned their backs on Canaan and are plunging again into the wilderness where they have been wandering for forty years. No wonder that we read: "The soul of the people was much discouraged because of the way."

For the people of God such an experience is not unusual. Because of discomforts and disappointments they often are disheartened. Yet such a condition is as dangerous as it is common. One who has lost hope is almost certain to be irritable, unreasonable, critical, complaining. "And the people spake against God, and against Moses, Wherefore have ye brought us up out of Egypt to die in the wilderness? for there is no bread, neither is there any water; and our soul loatheth this light bread."

This outcry was not unnatural or wholly without excuse. Their suffering was tragic; yet such a charge against God and against Moses was a grievous sin. By divine power they had been delivered from bitter bondage, and for long years had been sustained in the desert. The manna had become a monotonous diet. They were wearied of "this light bread," yet this had been supplied by daily miracle and it had supported the life of the people. The journey was long and dreary, but it was certain to bring them to Canaan. Their hearts should have been filled with gratitude. In any case, they should have turned to God with reverent petition. Their expression of discouragement was a pitiful sign of disloyalty to God. Discouragement usually so results. It complains of circumstances which are conditioned by divine providence. It is ready to repudiate the leading and the support which God provides; it forgets His mercy; it doubts His love and grace.

To bring one to repentance, to restore a right relation with God, often requires a severe remedy. "And the Lord sent fiery serpents among the people, and they bit the people; and much people of Israel died."

These serpents were named either from their bright color or from the burning pain of their poisonous bite. Their attack in appalling numbers need not be regarded as due to a miracle. The region was one which ever has been infested by serpents. Their venomous attack was an instrument which God employed to touch the hearts of His rebellious people. "Therefore the people came to Moses, and said, We have sinned, for we have spoken against the Lord, and against thee; pray unto the Lord, that he take away the serpents from us."

Such humble repentance and confession were not often shown by Israel. Whenever they are manifest they always are met by divine pardon and a message of peace. However, a mediator is necessary. The people turned to Moses as their intercessor. In spite of their disloyalty, "Moses prayed for the people." He was the type of the one Mediator between God and man, even our Saviour, "who ever lives to make intercession for us."

"And the Lord said unto Moses, Make thee a fiery serpent [an image of one], and set it upon a pole [standard]: and it shall come to pass that every one that is bitten, when he looketh upon it, shall live" [shall not die].

In obedience to this command "Moses made a serpent of brass," probably of brass or copper, because the color would resemble the appearance of a "fiery serpent." He "put it upon a pole," or a standard, so that it could be seen even from a distance. Then there followed the miraculous result which had been promised: "It came to pass, that if a serpent had bitten any man, when he beheld the serpent of brass, he lived." The cure was instantaneous, complete, permanent. As the result of a look a new life was given. It must have been a look of faith. However imperfect his understanding may have been, the one who looked must have had in mind the divine promise and must have trusted not in a lifeless image but in the gracious God who had provided such a marvelous cure. As an ancient teacher has said, "He that turned himself to it was not saved by the thing which he saw, but by Thee that art the Saviour of all."

This short story of the serpent of brass holds its immortal place in the literature of the world because of the use made of it by our Lord in His memorable dialogue with Nicodemus. The learned Jewish rabbi was surprised to hear that his own book of the Law contained in so brief a form the message of salvation which our Lord was eager to impart.

In interpreting the use which our Lord was making of this historic incident, we should observe: (1) Christ declared that in the brazen serpent one could find a type or symbol of the Saviour Himself. In such a comparison, however, one must be careful to avoid the least intimation that there was in Christ anything which a living serpent may represent. In Scripture, the serpent is ever a symbol for sin, insidious in its attack, crafty, cruel, and deadly in its venom. The serpent of brass was not a serpent. It was a mere image, just as Christ was made "in the likeness of sinful flesh" and for sin, but "in him was no sin."

(2) The serpent was "lifted up," so Christ was the crucified Saviour. He was God's provision for a sin-bitten race. His death was necessary, "so must the Son of man be lifted up."

(3) The condition of being cured was a "look" of faith. The Lord had said to Moses, "Every one that . . . looketh . . . shall live." Christ's parallel words were these, "Whosoever believeth . . . shall have everlasting life."

(4) The result of such a "look" was "life." **So a** vital trust in Christ and submission to His will and a determination to obey Him, result in "life eternal." This phrase does not mean merely an endless life but a kind of life, a life given by the spirit of God, and the life revealed in the Son of God.

Let us remember that one was cured, not by looking at his wound or by looking to his neighbor, or by trust in a lifeless image. No one is saved by looking at his sin, or by comparing himself with others, or by the power of any priest or sacrament or form. Faith is a personal and an individual experience. Each one who is conscious of sin, who confesses his helplessness, who turns to Christ in simple trust, will find the poison of sin arrested and will receive in its place an infusion of divine power and will enter on a new life which is the life "more abundant," which is "life indeed."

## THE JOURNEY TO MOAB [Ch. 21:10-35]

Israel, passing around the southern borders of Edom, and marching northward past the country of Moab, reaches the river Arnon, which runs from the highlands through a steep ravine to the "Salt Sea." It formed the border between Edom and Moab. Possibly the mention of this stream led the historian to quote the fragment of an ancient poem, said to be found "in the book of the wars of the Lord."

What he did in the Red sea,
And in the brooks of Arnon,

> And at the stream of the brooks
> That goeth down to the dwelling of Ar,
> And lieth upon the border of Moab (vs. 14, 15).

Even a more exact translation of the original Hebrew gives little clear meaning, other than to emphasize the location, at this time, of the armies of Israel. No one has any knowledge of the "book" to which reference is made. It is possible, however, that from the same source the fragment of another hymn is taken. It was written to celebrate the finding of water in a "well" (Hebrew "Beer") according to the promise of the Lord:

> Spring up, O well;
> Sing ye unto it:
> The princes digged the well,
> The nobles of the people digged it,
> By the direction of the lawgiver,
>     with their staves (vs. 17, 18).

The country beyond the Arnon was in control of the Amorites. Therefore, Moses sent messengers to Sihon, king of the Amorites, requesting permission for a peaceful passage through his land. The request was exactly the same as that which had been addressed to the king of Edom. The reply, however, was even more serious; it consisted in an armed attack in full force against the armies of Israel. There was no divine command to Moses to spare the enemy, as in the case of Edom. On the contrary, "Israel smote him with the edge of the sword, and possessed his land from Arnon unto Jabbok." Thus Sihon, who had conquered Moab, was himself overthrown, and his fall was commemorated in a notable Song of Triumph celebrating the victory of the Amorites over the Moabites (vs. 27-29) and then the triumph of Israel over the Amorites (v. 30):

> Come into Heshbon;
> Let the city of Sihon be built and prepared:
> For a fire is gone out of Heshbon,
> A flame from the city of Sihon:
> It hath consumed Ar of Moab,
> And the lords of the high places of Arnon.
>
> Woe to thee, Moab!
> Thou art undone, O people of Chemosh:
> He [that is Chemosh] hath given his sons as
>     fugitives,
> And his daughters into captivity,
> Unto Sihon, king of the Amorites.
>
> We have shot at them;
> Heshbon is perished even unto Dibon,
> And we have laid them waste even unto Nophah,
> Which reacheth unto Medeba.

The last four lines (v. 30) are supposed to be spoken by Israel, and may be translated:

> We cast them down into Dibon;
> We have wasted with fire
> Unto Nophah and Medeba;
> Heshbon is perished.

Thus Sihon was subdued, and Israel possessed the land as far north as the Jabbok. Beyond this river lay the territory of the giant Og, king of Bashan.

And the Lord said unto Moses, Fear him not: for I

have delivered him into thy hand, and all his people, and his land, and thou shalt do to him as thou didst unto Sihon king of the Amorites, which dwelt at Heshbon. So they smote him, and his sons, and all his people, until there was none left him alive: and they possessed his land (vs. 34, 35).

Therefore, all the territory east of the Jordan was in control of Moses and his victorious hosts. The long wilderness journey was ended. Israel was encamped on "the plains of Moab," ready, at last, to strike westward and to enter the Land of Promise.

## THE STORY OF BALAAM [Chs. 22-24]

A strange man was Balaam, the son of Beor of Pethor. He feared God and worshiped gold. He was a prophet of the Most High but was famed as a magician, a wizard, and a sorcerer. He pronounced blessings on the Israelites and then gave counsel by which they might be destroyed. He prayed that he might "die the death of the righteous," but ended his life in disaster and disgrace:

> To good and evil equal bent
> And both a devil and a saint.

These contradictions are easily explained. Balaam was attempting to serve two masters. His pitiful failure illustrated the solemn word of Christ, "Ye cannot serve God and mammon."

The home of Balaam was in the Euphrates valley, but his reputation had spread to distant lands. When the hosts of Israel had overwhelmed Sihon,

king of the Amorites, and Og, king of Bashan, and
had crossed the borders of Moab, the king of the
Moabites, Balak, the son of Zippor, was filled with
terror. He consulted the princes of Midian. They
agreed that it would be impossible to defeat the Israelites in battle but proposed that they might enlist
some magic power to weaken or turn back the threat-
ening foe. Therefore, they sent an embassy to Balaam
bearing rich "rewards of divination" with this request from Balak: "Come now therefore, I pray thee,
curse me this people; for they are too mighty for me:
peradventure I shall prevail, that we may smite them
out of the land: for I wot that he whom thou blessest
is blessed, and he whom thou cursest is cursed."

On their arrival at the home of Balaam the
sorcerer was delighted with the gift of gold, but uncertain as to the propriety of cursing the people of
God. He bade the ambassadors to wait until the
morning for his decision. Very properly he prayed
for light. When one is seeking to know the path of
right or wrong, he can rely absolutely on divine
guidance. The word which came to Balaam was definite and explicit, "Thou shalt not go with them; thou
shalt not curse the people: for they are blessed." In
the morning Balaam reported the message to the
princes of Balak but in rather different terms. "Get
you into your land," he said, "for the Lord refuseth
to give me leave to go with you." That is, "I should
like to go with you, but I am not allowed; I should
love to curse Israel, but I do not dare."

When one meets a temptation in that attitude
of mind he can be certain that the temptation will

return in a still more attractive form. So it was with Balaam. When Balak heard the reply of the double-minded prophet, he sent to Balaam more honorable princes and larger promises of promotion and honor, saying, "Come therefore, I pray thee, curse me this people." Balaam replies to the messengers with boastful bravery, "If Balak would give me his house full of silver and gold, I cannot go beyond the word of the Lord my God, to do less or more. Now therefore, I pray you, tarry ye also here this night, that I may know what the Lord will say unto me more." What "more" could the Lord say? Balaam knew perfectly well the will of the Lord. He seemed to hope that God might change His mind and that some circumstances might make it right to do what was wrong. He was tampering with his conscience, and, as is usually the result, his conscience was perverted. He adopted what he thought to be a compromise. He could not go and curse the people; but he believed he might go, even though it would be impossible to curse. God gave His permission but not His sanction. Balaam was allowed to go and to deliver a real message from God, but only to meet with greater temptation, with disappointment, with disgrace, with fatal failure. "There is a way which seemeth right unto a man, but the end thereof are the ways of death" (Prov. 14:12).

So Balaam started on his journey, anxious, irritable, uncertain. He is permitted to go but forbidden to accomplish the purpose of his journey. Furthermore, God gave to Balaam a gracious warning. He sent an angel with a drawn sword to stop the prophet on his mad mission. The ass on which Balaam was riding saw the angel, and three times attempted to turn aside or to escape. Balaam, more stupid than the beast, perceived no danger, and in anger beat the ass with his staff. Then the animal spoke to rebuke its senseless master. So Peter recalls this scene when describing certain false prophets of his own day: "Which have forsaken the right way, and are gone astray, following the way of Balaam the son of Beor, who loved the wages of unrighteousness; but was rebuked for his iniquity: the dumb ass speaking with man's voice forbad the madness of the prophet" (II Peter 2:15, 16).

At last the eyes of Balaam are open. He sees his peril; he recognizes his perversity. He admits that he has sinned, but he does not truly repent. He wishes to go forward but says to the angel, "Now therefore, if it displeases thee, I will get me back again." The old hypocrite knew that his course was displeasing to God and to His messenger, but still he was intent on his evil adventure. So he was allowed to go forward; he was used to pronounce a divine prophecy, but he was to meet his own doom. "And the angel of the Lord said unto Balaam, Go with the men: but only the word that I shall speak unto thee, that thou shalt speak."

"So Balaam went with the princes of Balak." The king came out to meet him in a city on the borders of Moab. He expressed regret that Balaam had delayed his coming, and renewed his promises of great reward. Balaam replies that he has gladly come but that he can say only what God puts in his mouth. He hopes the message will be a curse on Israel, but if not, his own reputation will be saved. He still will be regarded as a prophet of the Lord.

On the next day Balak accompanied by an imposing company of princes conducts Balaam to "the high places of Baal, that thence he might see the utmost part of the people" of Israel. Balaam now proposes an impressive ceremony which is to introduce the desired curse. The arrangement is to produce the semblance of a religious service. "Build me here seven altars," he commands, "and prepare me here seven oxen and seven rams; and Balak did as Balaam had spoken." Leaving Balak by the smoking altars, Balaam withdraws to a distance with the assumed secrecy of a great sorcerer. "Peradventure the Lord will come to meet me here," he says, "and whatsoever he sheweth me I will tell thee." God did meet Balaam, "and put a word in Balaam's mouth":

And he took up his parable, and said,
Balak the king of Moab hath brought me from Aram,
Out of the mountains of the east, saying,
Come, curse me Jacob,
And come, defy Israel.
How shall I curse, whom God hath not cursed?
Or how shall I defy, whom the Lord hath not defied?
For from the top of the rocks I see him,
And from the hills I behold him;
Lo, the people shall dwell alone,
And shall not be reckoned among the nations.
Who can count the dust of Jacob,
And the number of the fourth part of Israel?

Let me die the death of the righteous,
And let my last end be like his!

Balaam is astonished and disappointed by his own words. Balak is filled with disgust. He proposes that they go to another place from which they can view the hosts of Israel, which he hopes Balaam will curse. They go together to the top of Mount Pisgah and there repeat the ceremony of the seven altars and sacrifices. They seem to believe what so many people think is true, namely, that a thing which is morally wrong in one place may be innocent in another. The opening words of the next oracle rebuke this false sentiment.

God is not a man, that he should lie;
Neither the son of man, that he should repent:
Hath he said, and shall he not do it?
Or hath he spoken, and shall he not make it good?

The mind of God could not be changed by the altered location of the two conspirators. Balaam continues with his prophecy, speaking of God's grace and mercy toward the Israelites, and predicting great prosperity and power, which would lead to the conviction that this people was being divinely supported, so that it would be said of Jacob and Israel, "What hath God wrought!" Balak is bewildered. He requests that Balaam shall neither curse nor bless, and offers to bring Balaam to "another place," still believing that if they look down on Israel from a different angle it may be possible for Balaam to curse the people. Thus also many persons who are intent on doing evil insist that whether a thing is right or

wrong depends on the way in which one looks at it.
Balaam and Balak go together to the top of Mount
Peor, from which point they secure a view of the entire encampment of Israel. As Balaam looks down on
the orderly array of the Israelites, he cries out in
prophetic ecstasy:

> How goodly are thy tents, O Jacob,
> And thy tabernacles O Israel!

The oracle further predicts the future kingdom
of Israel. It describes the lionlike strength of the
people, and closes with the startling statement,

> Blessed is he that blesseth thee,
> And cursed is he that curseth thee.

Balak turns on Balaam in fierce anger: "I called
thee to curse mine enemies, and, behold, thou hast
altogether blessed them these three times. Therefore now flee thou to thy place." Balaam will not re-
tract his words. He reminds Balak that he had not
promised to curse Israel, but had warned Balak in
these words, "What the Lord saith that will I speak."
He refuses to be silent, and declares that in his part-
ing words he will declare to Balak what Israel will
do to the people of Moab in a later day.

> I shall see him, but not now:
> I shall behold him, but not nigh:
> There shall come a Star out of Jacob,
> And a Sceptre shall rise out of Israel,
> And shall smite the corners of Moab
> And destroy all the children of Sheth. . . .
> Out of Jacob shall come he that shall have dominion.

The precise king who may have been in the mind of Balaam it is impossible to conjecture. He is certainly predicting the conquest of Moab, and he continues to prophesy the defeat of the surrounding nations, such as Amalek, the Kenites, and even Asshur and Eber. Israel is to be victorious over all its enemies, and to enjoy the Land of Promise.

In the prediction of the "Star out of Jacob" and the "Sceptre out of Israel," the Jews have found a message of the Messiah, and Christians have seen a parable of a star which led out of the East wise men who differed greatly from the ancient sorcerer of Peor, and who were led to worship at the feet of the new-born King.

After pronouncing his four impressive parables or oracles "Balaam rose up and went and returned to his place." This, however, is not the end of the story. Other chapters in the ancient history tell us that Balaam was so disappointed, disgraced, and chagrined that he seeks to retrieve his fortune by giving to Balak advice which brings on Israel a calamity greater than any imagined curse. In the beginning of the story the miracle of a dumb beast speaking with man's voice was no greater than the miracle which was recorded as Balaam pronounced blessing on Israel. The beast spoke contrary to its nature, and Balaam spoke in direct opposition to his own purpose and desire, but what he had spoken was quite in accordance with the will of God.

However these marvelous prophecies may have been recorded or reported to Israel, they must have been a source of great encouragement. The people

as they were encamped on the plains of Moab stood
on the borders of the Land of Promise. There were
hard battles to be fought, but these noble prophecies,
so majestic in their form, so precise and arresting in
their contents, must have given new courage as they
predicted victory over all their enemies as the true
people of God.

## THE ZEAL OF PHINEHAS [Ch. 25]

One could wish that the story of Balaam ended
as the discredited sorcerer turned toward his home
in the East, but the inspired records give us a sad
sequel to his perverse endeavor to curse Israel. In
the disgraceful and shocking scenes depicted by the
present chapter, the sinister figure of Balaam looms
darkly in the background. As we read in the Apoc-
alypse, it was "Balaam who taught Balak to cast a
stumbling block before the children of Israel, to eat
things sacrificed unto idols and to commit fornica-
tion" (Rev. 2:14; Num. 31:16).

The facts seem to be that when he failed to win
the gold of Balak by disobeying God, when dismissed
by the king in dishonor and disgrace, Balaam was
maddened by disappointment and chagrin. He made
a last desperate effort to secure the rewards which
had been offered him. He gave to Balak satanic advice by which the people he had blessed might be
destroyed. He counseled the seduction of Israel by
enticing them to partake of the immoral rites of the
idolatrous Moabites and Midianites. The foul plot
was most successful. The Israelites "bowed down to

their gods," and there followed an obscene orgy of
unbridled license. The guilty people were visited by
a plague which resulted in the death of twenty-four
thousand. This plague was arrested only when sum-
mary vengeance had been inflicted on the offenders.
Moses gave the command that those who had led in
the idolatrous worship should be put to death. "The
judges of Israel" were commissioned to act for the
people in executing the guilty leaders. An example
of flagrant sin and its penalty was recorded in the
case of an Israelitish prince and the daughter of a
Midianitish chief. Their offense was flaunted publicly in the face of the stricken people. Phinehas, the
grandson of Aaron the priest, moved by fierce indig-
nation and acting in accordance with the command
of Moses, slew the two offenders with his own javelin.
Such a crude act of justice seemed to have been war-
ranted by the critical situation, for we read, "So the
plague was stayed from the children of Israel." The
deed of Phinehas met with divine approval. He was
given "the covenant of an eternal priesthood because
he was zealous for his God and made an atonement
for the children of Israel."

A still wider decree of vengeance was pronounced on those who had enticed Israel to sin.
Moses was told to "vex the Midianites and smite
them." These were stern and cruel days, but it can
be understood that, as Israel was taking possession of
a new home and was to be surrounded by idolatrous
peoples, they needed to be warned of the perils which
would beset them. Just as the prophecies of Balaam
had encouraged the Israelites as they were about to

enter the Land of Promise, so these shocking events of Baal-Peor impressed on the people the danger of uniting with their neighbors in idol worship and practice.

But what was the fate of Balaam? Evidently his course was visited with just retribution. Found among the enemies of Israel in the ranks of the defeated Midianites, of him the historian makes this brief and pathetic entry, "Balaam the son of Beor, they slew with the sword" (Num. 31:8). He once had sighed to "die the death of the righteous," but then he bartered his soul for a purse of gold. His epitaph may be recorded in the words of the apostle: "Balaam, the son of Beor, who loved the wages of unrighteousness" (II Peter 2:15).

## THE SECOND CENSUS [26:1-51]

Some forty years have passed since the numbering of the people at Mount Sinai, just as the wilderness journey was to begin. Now that journey has ended, and the hosts of Israel are encamped "on the plains of Moab, by Jordan near Jericho." They are about to enter Canaan, and this was the occasion for a second census.

The figures are much the same, with a sum total of over six hundred thousand. Seven of the tribes have increased in numbers, five report a reduced enrollment. They are named in the same order, except that Manasseh has become larger than Ephraim and is listed before its kindred tribe. The great loss has been sustained by Simeon; possibly it suffered most from the plague which came as a punishment on Zimri, a chief offender, whose fault may have been shared by his fellow tribesmen.

There was, however, an appalling contrast between the first and second muster rolls of the army of the Israelites. Only two names, Joshua and Caleb, appear on both lists of warriors. More than six hundred thousand had perished; their "bodies fell in the wilderness." "They were unable to enter" the Land of Promise "because of unbelief." Their tragic fate became for all future years a solemn warning against apostasy and disobedience to God (Heb. 3:7-9; Jude 5).

Yet this second numbering did not look to the past, but to the future. It was not strictly a census. It was the muster of an army. Except the Levites, it enrolled only those men who were twenty years old and upward; they must be prepared for battle. The Midianites were to be subdued; Canaan was to be won by conquest.

The people of God are never exempt from struggle. Faith is absolutely necessary, but it must be expressed in determination and action. Past failure should inspire present resolution and future trust.

There was another reason for this census. The land, when conquered, was to be divided among the tribes, the amount of territory to be proportioned to the size of the tribe. It was thus necessary to have on record the exact enrollment which this "numbering" supplied.

A still further purpose looks to the more distant future. Before Israel there lay a great destiny. The people needed to be united and distinct from the nations of the world. To this end genealogies needed to be regarded as sacred and to be carefully preserved. Each Hebrew was taught to look with pride on his descent from Abraham and Isaac and Jacob, and to look forward to the fulfilment of great promises, which would give to Israel a unique place in the history of the world. These lists of names and families, which discourage the reading of books like Numbers, are not of equal historic or spiritual value to some other portions of Scripture, but they have their function in the inspired word and in the economy of God.

## THE INHERITANCE OF WOMEN [Ch. 27:1-11]

Not all persons realize what has been done for the emancipation and elevation of woman by the Hebrew-Christian tradition and practice. One important example is given by the incident connected with the five daughters of Zelophehad. They came to Moses and the princes representing "all the congregation," at the place of solemn assembly, requesting that they should be granted the inheritance of their father. They were not asking for property their father previously had held. The Land of Promise was to be conquered and divided among the tribes and specifically among the men of each tribe. These daughters were requesting that, as their father had died leaving no sons, the portion which would have been assigned to him might be promised to them. It was an act of faith. They believed in the future victory of Israel; they trusted the honor and justice of Moses. Their request was strengthened by the plea that their father had not been implicated in the rebellion of Korah, or in any other criminal course which would have deprived his descendants of their inheritance. He "had died in his own sin," meaning that he shared only the common condemnation, resting on the older generation, to be excluded from the Land of Promise. The new generation was to enter the land, and these daughters were claiming the inheritance which, had he lived, their father would have received.

The question was serious. The problem was new. Moses sought divine guidance. He received the definite reply: "Thou shalt cause the inheritance of their father to pass unto them." The faith of these noble women was rewarded, not only by the fulfilment of their desire, but by the further enactment that, henceforth, in all families, where there were no sons, the daughters should inherit, and where there were no daughters, then the nearest relatives of the father should be the legal heirs. This statement of the equal rights of women was in accord with the future legislation of all enlightened nations.

## THE APPOINTMENT OF JOSHUA [Ch. 27:12-23]

To a great leader who is compelled to relinquish his task, it always must be a comfort and consolation to know that a worthy successor has been appointed who is certain to carry out his plans and to complete his work. So it was with Moses. The picture of his death is dark with shadows of disappointment and regret. However, the gloom is somewhat dispelled by the radiant spirit of the great leader and by the assurance that Joshua is appointed to take his place.

He is bidden to climb to the summit of Mount Abarim where he can catch a glimpse of the land on which the hopes of his life have been centered, and on the border of which he is now to die. He is reminded that his death is the penalty for his moral failure at Kadesh. Possibly he learns the meaning of the solemn phrase, "The sting of death is sin." Yet, not a murmur falls from his lips. He seems utterly forgetful of self. His whole thought is for the welfare of the people to whom he has devoted his life, the people whose ingratitude and rebellion had been more than even his patience and meekness could endure. For them he prays, not for himself. He pleads that a leader may be chosen for them, "that the congregation of the Lord be not as sheep which have no shepherd." This choice he leaves to the Lord. How deeply gratifying to learn that the divine selection is one he himself would have made! Indeed, who else than Joshua, the son of Nun, could have followed Moses as the leader of Israel? Here was one of the only two living men who had known the anguish of Egypt, the trials of the desert, and had visited the Land of Promise. Joshua had been entrusted by Moses to command the armies in the first great battle. He had secured a notable victory on the plain, while Moses, Aaron, and Hur interceded with God on the mountain. For nearly forty years he had been the lieutenant of Moses, his assistant, his friend.

He was a great soldier, and at the same time a man of God. He was modest, courageous, gentle, unselfish and just. He seems to have been qualified and trained for his great task as the conqueror of Canaan.

No faults are recorded in the story of his distinguished career. In one point, however, he was less favored than his great commander. Moses was granted a mysterious but real access to the presence of God to receive divine guidance. Joshua, on the other hand, was to consult with Eleazar the priest, who would communicate to him the will of the Lord as to the movement of the armies of Israel.

With this understanding, Moses placed Joshua "before Eleazar the priest, and before all the congregation; and he laid his hands upon him," by this symbolic act indicating that all the responsibilities of leadership were now transferred by Moses to his successor; and he "gave him a charge," an encouraging message of affection, of counsel and farewell. Then Moses ascended the mountain, to be seen no more of men, until that memorable day, when, inside the Promised Land, on the slopes of Hermon, he appeared in glory with the transfigured Christ, of whom, as the great prophet, he had been a figure and a type.

## Offerings and Vows [Chs. 28 to 30]

The "church year," or "Christian year," may be associated in thought with the sacred year of the Hebrews. Both have been open to abuse by affording an opportunity for the unwarranted multiplication of burdensome rites and ceremonies and feasts and fasts; yet both have proved helpful to the people of God by reminding them, at stated periods, of their dependence on Him and their duties and privileges as His worshipers.

The laws recorded in Numbers 28 and 29 are designed to specify the exact offerings to be presented at each one of the sacred seasons, but in naming these offerings there is a more detailed and connected account of these "set times of Jehovah" than can be found in any other portion of Scripture. It comprises a brief and orderly statement of Israel's sacred year.

The offerings here specified were to be presented at a central place of worship in the name of the whole congregation. Individual worshipers might bring their own similar offerings at various times and as circumstances might suggest.

The nature and meaning of these offerings have been set forth in Leviticus (Chs. 1 to 7), and the sacred year outlined (Chs. 23 to 25). The sacrifices and the stated seasons, more completely outlined here, were designed to signify that the possessions and the time of the worshipers belonged wholly to the Lord.

First of all were the *daily* offerings—"the morning and the evening sacrifice." In each case two spotless yearling lambs were presented as a "burnt-offering," accompanied by a "meal offering" of flour mixed with oil and a "drink offering" of wine. The "burnt offering" was the symbol of complete dedication, and the "meal" and "drink" offerings were tokens of gratitude. Thus the priests, at the place of worship, representing the entire congregation, gave thanks for the gifts and mercies of each succeeding day, and dedicated the people to the service of God. At the time of such public sacrifices individual worshipers were expected to present their offerings of praise and devotion. Probably this was neglected by many. By others, however, prayers and thanksgiving were offered three times or even seven times a day. The followers of Christ, as a precious custom, have selected the morning and the evening as fitting times for worship and praise.

This daily service was the foundation of the entire sacrificial system of the Hebrews; whatever else was offered was regarded as in addition and not in place of it. The people were thus taught to regard every day as sacred. All distinction between days was temporary and arbitrary. This was emphasized in the teachings of Paul (Rom. 14:5, 6. Gal. 4:10. Col. 2:16, 17).

One day in seven, however, was marked by special sacrifices. These were the *Sabbath* offerings. They consisted of two lambs, with the accompanying "meal" or "drink" offerings; yet these were merely supplements to the invariable "morning and evening sacrifices." They did emphasize the special sanctity of the day. Such sacrifices are mentioned here for the first time. Sabbath observance, however, had previously been established by the Law (Ex. 20:10) and given solemn sanction by the punishment of an offender (Ch. 15:32-36). The Sabbath remains as the one day which the Christian is required to regard as sacred, not only because of ancient law, but also because of the example and precept of Christ. As "Lord of the Sabbath" He taught His followers, by precept and example, to observe the day as a period of worship, and of rest to be broken only by deeds of necessity and mercy. As it is now a memorial of His resurrection, Christians should be the more eager to regard it as the very "day of days."

For the first time, here also, mention is made of the offerings in observance of the *New Moon*. In addition to a "burnt offering" of two young bullocks, a ram and seven lambs, and meal and drink offerings, a kid was presented as a "sin offering." These sacrifices were accompanied by the sounding of the Silver Trumpets (Ch. 10:10), which gave a festal air to the occasion. Thus joyfully was consecrated to God, not only each day, and each week, but each recurring month.

Likewise, the *year* was dedicated to God by a series of annual festivals which were to be observed each with its prescribed offerings. These festivals were in two groups, one in the spring and another in the autumn. On "the fourteenth day of the first month" (about our March-April) was observed "the *Passover*," inseparable from "the feast of *Unleavened Bread*," which feast continued for seven days, beginning with the "fifteenth day of this month." Thus was commemorated the birth of a nation; for this celebration called to mind the night on which the angel of death passed over the houses of the Israelites, when the stricken Egyptians besought the people to leave the land of bondage, when the departure was in such haste that the bread was taken before it had time to be leavened. Strictly speaking, Passover was more like a sacrament than a feast. The day ended with the great Supper, when all worshipers partook of a lamb, recalling the sprinkled blood which had given security from the destroying angel on the night of the exodus. During the following seven days a glad feast was enjoyed, beginning and ending with a day of "holy convocation." On pain of death all leaven was excluded from the homes of the people, the unleavened bread then eaten giving its name to the feast.

The offerings of each day were the same as those prescribed for the feast of the New Moon; however, of all the sacrifices the "paschal lamb" held the place of supreme importance. Saint Paul makes use of these historic types when he insists that all who accept Christ as a divine Sacrifice for sin must exclude from their lives all "leaven," which is a symbol of evil: "For even Christ our Passover is sacrificed for us: therefore let us keep the feast, not with old leaven, neither with the leaven of malice and wickedness; but with the unleavened bread of sincerity and truth" (I Cor. 5:7, 8).

Fifty days after presenting to the Lord a sheaf of ripened grain at the time of Passover came *Pentecost* (Greek "fiftieth"). This was called also the "Feast of Weeks," as it was measured by the passing of seven weeks after the first great annual festival. It was also named the "Feast of Harvest," or the "Day of First-fruits," because, in addition to the sacrifices prescribed for the previous feasts, two loaves of bread were presented to the Lord as the firstfruits of the grain harvest which now was complete.

In the Christian year, Easter is made to correspond to Passover, commemorating, as it does, the great redemption accomplished by the risen Christ; and Pentecost, or "Whitsunday," is taken as the antitype of the Hebrew "Feast of Harvest"; for, fifty days after the resurrection, by the manifested power of the Holy Spirit, a great harvest of souls was brought into living fellowship with Christ and bound into one Body, the Church of Christ. These were the firstfruits of the great harvest still being garnered by the power of the same Spirit wherever Christ is proclaimed.

As the Seventh Day and the Seventh Week, so the Seventh Month was marked by prescribed offerings to indicate that it was a sacred season, when the people could express their gratitude to God and the devotion to Him of their time as well as their possessions. The month opened with the *Feast of Trumpets.* The sacrifices were more numerous than on the other occasions, and the joyful character of the feast and of the month then ushered in was signified by the more than usual sounding of the silver trumpets, a custom which gave its name to this festal day.

The general joyous character of the month was interrupted by the ceremonies of *Great Day of Atonement.* These were appointed for the "tenth day" of the month. This was a day of national humiliation, of penitence and of pardon. There was to be a holy convocation. No servile work was to be done. The people were to "afflict" their souls, probably by a most rigid fast. The offerings and the elaborate ritual of the day made prominent the work of the Great High Priest (Lev. 16), the symbolism of which finds its fulfilment in the priesthood and atonement of Christ, set forth in impressive detail in the Epistle to the Hebrews.

The culmination and most joyous festival of the sacred year was found in the *Feast of Tabernacles.* This was named from the custom of dwelling, during the days of the festival, in huts and booths, usually constructed from the boughs and branches of trees. The purpose was to recall the life of the wilderness sojourn, but more particularly to rejoice in the completion of the harvest, when all the products of field and orchard and vineyard had been garnered. For this reason it was called also the "Feast of Ingathering," which was in the nature of a "Harvest Home" festival.

The feast began on the fifteenth day of the seventh month (about our October) and continued for seven days. It was a season of thanksgiving, of joy and gladness. This was followed by an "eighth day," when a "solemn assembly" marked the close, not only of the feast, but also of the completed round of annual festivals.

The offerings made during the week of Tabernacles were unequaled in number, including seventy bullocks, fourteen rams, and ninety-six lambs. Of these bullocks, thirteen were offered on the first day of the feast, one less on each following day until, on the seventh day, seven were offered, making seventy in all. Thus stress was laid on the sacred symbolic number "seven" in recognition of the covenant with God. Indeed, all these multiplied offerings were designed to express gratitude and consecration. In addition to those here specified for the congregation, it must be remembered that individual sacrifices were being presented, namely, those connected with "vows and freewill offerings, and meal offerings, and drink offerings, and peace offerings" (Ch. 29:39).

It will be obvious that in all the ritual for the "set times" of worship here outlined (Chs. 28, 29) the supreme feature is that of the offerings. Also, among the sacrifices, while the "sin offering" is never omitted, the chief prominence is that of the burnt offering and the meal offering. The supreme message here is not that of atonement, but of gratitude and of dedication to God. So when the type is fulfilled in the supreme Offering, one is pointed to Christ, not only as the "divine sacrifice for sin, but also as an ensample of holy living." The Christian reader is reminded of the words of Paul: "I beseech you therefore, brethren, by the mercies of God, that ye present your bodies, a living sacrifice, holy, acceptable unto God, which is your reasonable service. And be not conformed to this world: but be ye transformed by the renewing of your mind, that ye may prove what is that good, and acceptable, and perfect, will of God" (Rom. 12:1, 2).

The *law of vows* recorded in Chapter 30, in addition to the legislation of Leviticus 27, should be emphasized in these days when the sanctity of vows is being so flagrantly disregarded. It should be remembered that vows of marriage, of church membership, of baptism, of ordination, and similar pledges, involve solemn obligations not merely to men but to God. The general principle is clearly stated. Two words for vows are here employed, indicating obligation to do something for God and also to refrain from some privilege or enjoyment. In both cases the promise must be fulfilled. "If a man vow a vow unto the Lord, or swear an oath to bind his soul with a bond; he shall not break his word, he shall do according to all that proceedeth out of his mouth" (Ch. 30:2).

Our Saviour did not forbid assuming the obligation of a sacred vow. He indicated that in ordinary conversation and in common transactions, vows and oaths should not be necessary nor be rashly pronounced. Among his followers promises were to be kept, and were to need no further sanction: "Let your communication be Yea, yea; Nay, nay: for whatsoever is more than these cometh of evil" (Matt. 5:37).

Furthermore our Lord rebuked the sophistry of the Jews and rabbis of his day by which solemn vows were evaded and declared to be void (Matt. 5:31, 32; 15:4-9).

The law of Moses dealt specifically with the vows of women. Four cases are mentioned: (1) an unmarried woman living in the home of her father; (2) a woman who marries with an unfulfilled vow resting on her; (3) the vow of a widow or of a woman who has been divorced; (4) the vow of a married woman.

In the first case the vow was binding only when it was known and sanctioned by the father. In the second case the vow was void unless allowed by the future husband. The vows of widows or divorced women could not be disregarded. As for married women, it was enacted: "Every vow and every binding oath to afflict the soul, her husband may establish it, or her husband may make it void."

These regulations not only enforced the sacredness of vows, but established the headship of the father or the husband in matters of religion, and safeguarded the unity and the peace of the family. In their religious zeal women might make pledges which were unwise or too generous to be paid. Of this the father or husband could be the judge. Vows are obligations to God voluntarily assumed; they must not, however, be such as to involve the security or comfort of other persons whose permission has not been granted.

## THE WAR AGAINST MIDIAN [Ch. 31]

The war against Midian was in the nature of a punitive expedition. In it only a limited number of Israelites were engaged, and it resulted in the destruction of only a portion of the Midianites. Of the Israelites, one thousand were selected from each tribe, merely twelve thousand from the hosts, which numbered more than six hundred thousand. As for the Midianites, it is evident that the entire nation was not destroyed, for at a later period, in the days of the Judges, Midianites swarmed over the land of Canaan like an army of locusts.

However, the Midianites had been guilty of

grievous fault and the penalty visited upon them was not undeserved. Following the vile counsel of Balaam, the women of Midian had seduced the people of Israel to take part in the idolatrous and lascivious rites of Baal-Peor. In the consequent plague twenty-four thousand Israelites perished.

It was then decreed that the Midianites should be "vexed and smitten" (Ch. 25:17), that is, regarded as enemies and treated with severity. The time for such retribution had arrived. Israel was about to enter the Land of Promise. It was absolutely necessary for the preservation of morality and religion that the people should be protected from the contagion and corruption of such neighbors and foes. Believing in the divine sanction, the warriors went forth to the sound of the silver trumpets and accompanied by the son of the high priest. The Midianites, apparently surprised, offered feeble resistance. Their entire force was killed or taken captive, together with vast herds of cattle and enormous amounts of booty. Only the lives of the younger women were spared. According to the brief and tragic report, "Balaam also the son of Beor they slew with the sword."

This was a distressing episode. It must be understood, not as an act of revenge, but as a terrible moral as well as a military necessity. However, all who had killed any of the enemy or touched a dead body were regarded as unclean. They were excluded from the camp of Israel for seven days; on the third day and on the seventh day they and all the captives submitted to rites of purification. The booty like-

wise was purified by fire or by the "water of separation."

As for the booty, it was divided equally between
those who had gone forth to battle and those who had
remained in the camp. The warriors then paid a trib-
ute to the priests; it consisted of one out of every
five hundred captives or animals. The people contributed one out of fifty, which was given to the Levites. A special gift was presented by the officers of
the army "to make atonement for their souls before
the Lord." This gift was in the nature of a thank
offering in recognition of the providential preservation of their lives.

This story of Midian is painful but not without
its message. War is always a scourge and a curse; but
there are some worse things. One is slavery; another
is uncontrolled and incurable immorality.

### SETTLEMENT EAST OF THE JORDAN [Ch. 32]

Now that the nations dwelling to the east of the
river Jordan have been conquered, it is not surprising that certain tribes of Israel desire to take possession of this land at once. It was the region, north
and south of the Jabbok, commonly associated with
the name of Gilead, rich in agriculture and of fertile
soil. "The children of Reuben and the children of
Gad" possessed great herds of cattle. Seeing the character of the land, they came to Moses and the other
rulers with the request, "Let the land be given unto
thy servants for a possession, and bring us not over
Jordan." This petition did not show disloyalty on

the part of the two tribes, nor was it prompted merely by the desire to escape from further warfare; however, it is difficult to defend these petitioners from the charge of selfishness. They certainly had a regard for their own interest rather than the interests of the nation which faced the necessity of conquering the land of Canaan.

In any case, Moses meets the request with a sharp rebuke: "Shall your brethren go to war, and shall ye sit here? And wherefore discourage ye the heart of the children of Israel from going over into the land which the Lord hath given them?" He recalls the fact that once before the people had reached the borders of the Land of Promise, but had been discouraged by some of their own number, and had been turned back to wander for forty years in the wilderness and there to die. These tribes would be guilty of the same offense, if they now deserted their fellow Israelites who were about to begin the conquest of the land.

The justice of the rebuke was realized. The tribes of Reuben and Gad offered to provide for the safety of their families and their cattle and then to cross the Jordan and to fight for their brethren, even to go in the very van of the forces until the conquest of Canaan was complete.

This offer Moses accepts, but with the solemn warning that the promise must be kept faithfully. If not, the time would come when they would need the help of their brethren against the enemies from the north and east: "And be sure your sin will find you out."

The two tribes renew their pledge: "We will pass over armed before the Lord into the land of Canaan, that the possession of our inheritance on this side Jordan may be ours." They proved faithful to their promise, and fought valiantly for the conquest of the land west of the Jordan, and then returned triumphantly to their allotted home in "Gilead," east of the Jordan.

It is not difficult to point the lesson that the people of God should ever be ready to help and strengthen and support their fellow warriors in the struggle against evil and entrenched wrong. Also it may be noted that the apparent selfishness, which led the tribes to consider first their own interests, met with the natural result; they always were most exposed to attack from hostile forces and were the first of the tribes to be carried captive. Selfishness is sure to expose one to moral perils and in the end results in its own defeat.

The story closes with the allotment to "the half tribe of Manasseh" of territory to the north of Reuben and Gad. The reason for this assignment was the principal part played by representatives of Manasseh in the conquest of this particular region east of the Jordan. Thus was begun the settlement of the Children of Israel in the land of their long expectations and their hopes.


## THE WILDERNESS ENCAMPMENTS [Ch. 33:1-49]

The Book of Numbers, as will be remembered, is a record of the wilderness experiences of the

Twelve Tribes of Israel on their migration from
Egypt to Canaan. The writer did not interrupt his
narrative even to name all the places where the tribes
encamped but mentioned only those stopping places
where important events occurred. As he brings the
story to a close, it is natural, therefore, that he should
renew the wilderness wanderings by giving an exact
itinerary of the journeys and should mention in order all the encampments of Israel. This itinerary
does not include all their possible stopping places,
but those sites where the tabernacle was erected and
the people were located for longer periods.

This list of names includes forty-two stations.
Of these, eighteen are mentioned nowhere else. To
identify these locations is not always possible, nor is
it necessary. Yet even a cursory reading of this chapter deepens the impression of the historical and relia-
ble character of the book. Furthermore, it intimates
the deep interest in His people which was felt by
their Redeemer and Lord. He knew every stage of
their pilgrimage. It was by His command that Moses
wrote these "goings out according to their journeys."
That is, he recorded these "encampments." It is,
then, not too much to say that the review of such a
bare list of names may remind one that "the Lord
knows them that are his," and "will preserve their
going out and their coming in," for "he that keepeth
Israel shall neither slumber nor sleep" (vs. 1, 2).

To his itinerary the writer adds no historical
notes, with two posible exceptions. First, in speaking
of the escape from bondage and the beginning of the
wilderness journeys, it is stated that "the children of

Israel went out with an high hand in the sight of all the Egyptians, for the Egyptians *were burying* all their first-born." Those who remember how intensely the Egyptians were concerned with funeral rites may conclude properly that this is one explanation of why the Israelites escaped from Egypt that night with so little opposition (vs. 3, 4).

For the most part, the stations mentioned between Egypt and Sinai are identified with events recorded in the Book of Exodus (vs. 5-15).

From Sinai to Rithmah (probably "Kadesh") was a short journey (vs. 16-18), and it was from this place on the borders of Canaan that because of their unbelief the tribes had been driven back to wander for thirty-seven years in the wilderness. For all these years only eighteen encampments are recorded (vs. 19-36), possibly indicating that, for the most part, the people were scattered in search of water and pasturage, and gathered only in an ordered encampment around the tabernacle at the places recorded. The only note of history during the last year of the wanderings was the death of Aaron at Mount Hor (vs. 37-39).

When, at last, the people had reached "the plains of Moab by Jordan near Jericho," and had "pitched by Jordan" (vs. 48, 49), the Lord gave to Moses a stern command concerning the conquest of Canaan. The Israelites were to "drive out all the inhabitatnts of the land," they were to destroy all their idols and places of idol worship, and were to divide the land by lot among the tribes, according to their relative size. In case they failed, the people who were allowed to remain in the land would prove to be "pricks in their eyes and thorns in their sides."

The further divine warning was added, "Moreover it shall come to pass that I shall do unto you, as I thought to do unto them." It was a difficult task which was assigned to Israel. Never was it completely accomplished. They allowed idolators to remain in the land; they were "vexed by them," and, finally, they were "driven out" of their land by Assyria and Babylon, as the Canaanites should have been by the conquering tribes of Israel (vs. 50-56).


## The Allotment of the Land [Ch. 34]

Now the boundaries of the land promised to Israel are defined more exactly and further instructions are given as to its division. The territory is popularly known as Canaan, although held in different parts and at various times by nations other than the Canaanites (Ex. 23:23). The land lay between the Mediterranean Sea and the river Jordan. The length was about one hundred and eighty miles, and the breadth measured on an average forty miles. To this territory, just before the conquest by Israel, was added the region of Gilead and Bashan, on the east side of the Jordan. These two territories made up the Holy Land, the limits of which were recognized commonly until the overthrow of the Jewish state. In the time of David and Solomon the Hebrew dominion extended as far south as the Red Sea, and to the east as far as the river Euphrates. Such a dominion, as thus finally realized, had been promised while Israel was still encamped at Sinai (Ex. 23:31).

However, when now on the plains of Moab, and about to enter the Land of Promise, Moses describes with great exactness the country to be conquered. The southern boundary extended from the lowest extremity of the Dead Sea westward through Kadesh-Barnea to the "River of Egypt," not the Nile, but a small stream emptying into the Mediterranean. This "Great Sea" formed the western boundary. The northern boundary is less easily understood, but is described as extending from a point on the Mediterranean, marked by "Mount Hor" (probably Mount Lebanon) eastward to the "entrance of Hamath," and thirty miles farther to Zedad. It is difficult to identify these landmarks; but, starting southward, the natural eastern border was the Sea of Galilee, the valley of the Jordan and the Dead Sea.

These exact boundaries of the land, as laid down by Moses, had a definite purpose. Israel was not to enter on a career of unlimited conquest, but was to occupy a restricted country to which no nation had a more rightful claim. It was to seek no further territory but was to accomplish peacefully its destiny, separated from surrounding idolators, and preserving the knowledge and the worship of the one living and true God.

For the *division* of this land *among* the *tribes* according to their size, some provision already had been made by the census recently taken. The exact numbers of each tribe had been carefully recorded.

A further provision was made by Moses in appointing a commission which could accomplish the task of justly alloting the territory. This commission was headed by Eleazar the high priest and Joshua the commander of the armies; it included one "prince" from each of the ten tribes, except those to which land east of the Jordan had been granted. The relative positions of the various inheritances were to be determined by lot, but their dimensions were to be proportioned to the numbers of each tribe as determined by the census. The names of the ten commissioners are unfamiliar, except that of Caleb of the tribe of Judah. The appointment of such representatives would assure fairness in the division of the country which was to be conquered.

The land of Canaan has been used by the Christian Church, in sermon and in song, as a symbol both of the present experiences of the followers of Christ and also of their future glory. As the Israelites did not complete their conquest, either by taking possession of all the territory allotted to them, or by utterly subduing the idolatrous inhabitants, so, too, Christians are ever failing to enjoy all the blessedness offered to them, and are never completely defeating the indwelling enemies of their souls. However, they expect to enter on a heavenly Canaan and ultimately to enjoy the "rest that remaineth for the people of God." Yet, whether they achieve present victories, or look forward to "the inheritance of the saints in light," all that is granted them is ascribed to Him who is at once their Great High Priest and the Captain of their Salvation.

## CITIES OF REFUGE [Ch. 35]

When directions had been given for the division of the land among the conquering tribes, it was necessary that provision should be made for the Levites, whose duties were religious and who therefore would have no part in the task of conquest.

Therefore Moses, under divine guidance, commanded that forty-eight cities should be assigned to the tribe of Levi as their places of residence. These cities should be scattered throughout the territory of the other tribes in proportion to the population. To the Levites were to be granted also "suburbs," or fields adjacent to the cities, "for their cattle," and for all their substance (or "for their sheep and goats") and "for all their beasts." In each case the "suburb" was to be in the form of a hollow square two thirds of a mile in each direction; each side was to be one third of a mile beyond the city wall. While such farm land would suffice for pasturage, it would not be extensive enough to furnish a livelihood by agriculture. The Levites were supported largely by the tithes contributed by the members of the other tribes. Nothing is said about the actual duties of the Levites in connection with their residence in the cities assigned. They probably performed religious functions and instructed the people in the Law, even while living at a distance from the appointed places of worship. It seems, also, that they were not the exclusive residents of these cities, and thus, as representatives of religion, they were kept in close contact with the people of other tribes.

From these forty-eight cities, three were selected on each side of the Jordan as *cities* of *refuge*. To one of these cities any person who unintentionally or without enmity had killed a fellow Israelite might flee and remain in safety until his innocence could be determined by a court of justice. These cities were not intended to afford an asylum for those guilty of murder "with malice aforethought"; nor could any fine be accepted to secure pardon for such a crime. The law was stern and relentless: "The murderer shall surely be put to death" (v. 16).

In connection with the provision of these "cities of refuge" a custom is mentioned which may have been one reason for their establishment. According to this custom the nearest kinsman of a murdered man had the right of avenging his blood. Such a custom was open to severe abuse. The one charged with the crime might have no opportunity of establishing his innocence; the "avenger" might act in ignorance, with haste, or when blinded by hate. To mitigate such evils was the object of establishing these places of safety: "They shall be unto you cities of refuge from the avenger; that the manslayer die not, until he stand before the congregation in judgment" (v. 12).

However, one who had killed a fellow man was not regarded as wholly faultless. He might flee for safety to the city of refuge, but he must remain there "until the death of the high priest." Even when he had been adjudged innocent he could leave the city only at his own peril. He was a virtual prisoner. As an exile from home, he could not cultivate his ancestral fields nor enjoy the fellowship of his family and friends. Yet, on "the death of the high priest" all restrictions were removed. He could return to his possession under the protection of the law.

No doubt moral and spiritual lessons can be drawn from this provision for the "Cities of Refuge"; yet, in seeking here for types and symbols, one needs to exercise caution and reserve. It is, however, quite natural that the "death of the high priest" is regarded by many as a faint prophetic shadow of the spiritual deliverance which has followed upon the atoning death of our Lord. Also, by way of contrast, there has been found, at the foot of the Cross, a sure place of refuge for those who have been guilty, not of one form of sin, but of every form of transgression and fault.

## TRIBAL INHERITANCE [Ch. 36]

The directions were now complete for the division of the Land of Promise among the Tribes of Israel. This division was to be made by lot according to their numbers, and under the supervision of the special commission appointed by Moses. All this was in accordance with a divine command, and the boundaries of the territories allotted to the tribes were to be permanent.

A recent ordinance, however, threatened to produce confusion and to break down tribal lines, and to make it possible for an Israelite belonging to one tribe to possess land within the boundaries of another tribe. This ordinance had been established at the request of the daughters of Zelophehad (Ch. 27:1-11). Their father had died leaving no sons; therefore, when the matter had been presented to Moses, he was divinely guided to declare that in such cases the daughters should inherit the estate of their father.

The daughters in question belonged to the tribe of Manasseh. The problem was then presented: in case these daughters married men from other tribes, would they take their right of inheritance with them? Would their husbands, belonging to various tribes, then own land within the boundaries of Manasseh? If so, and if the land should be sold, would not the loss to this tribe be made permanent by the coming of the year of Jubilee? On such a year the land would be returned to the husband or to his heirs and would forever be lost to the tribe to which the daughters of Zelophehad belonged.

To meet this problem it was enacted that, while daughters might inherit property, no heiress could marry outside the circle of her relatives. Thus no man could become the possessor of land beyond the boundaries of his own tribe, and thus the tribal division of the land was made permanent.

Whatever may be thought of the wisdom or justice of so limiting the freedom of an heiress, it was regarded as necessary thus to preserve the continuance of family titles and the unity of the nation. Israel was the people of God. It had a unique mission; it must be kept distinct from surrounding nations; and each of its tribes needed to be kept strong and to remain conscious of its traditions and heritage and hopes. The union of such tribes made for the more vital union and strength of the nation.

This provision for tribal inheritance is quite in the spirit of the Book of Numbers. Here each individual, each family, each tribe is enrolled. Every Israelite is made conscious of a noble heritage from the past, and the promise of a great inheritance in the future is given him. In a figurative sense, all who belong to the "family of the redeemed" have an abiding inheritance. Their "names are written in heaven." They are "heirs of God and joint heirs with Jesus Christ."